The Right Fit

An Educator's
Career Handbook
and Employment
Guide

The Right Fit
An Educator's Career Handbook and Employment Guide

Judy A. Strother
California State University–Fullerton

Darrel R. Marshall
University of Arizona

GSP

Gorsuch Scarisbrick, Publishers
Scottsdale, Arizona

Editor: John Gorsuch
Production Manager: Carol Hunter
Interior Design: Shadow Canyon Graphics
Cover Design: Kathy Feeney/Graphics 2
Typesetter: Shadow Canyon Graphics

Gorsuch Scarisbrick, Publishers
8233 Via Paseo del Norte, Suite F-400
Scottsdale, Arizona 85258

10 9 8 7 6 5 4 3 2 1

ISBN 0-89787-814-0

About the Authors

Judy Strother is a community college counselor and university instructor. She holds two Master of Arts Degrees, one in Education Instruction and Curriculum and another in Career Counseling. Her extensive professional background includes over 19 years of teaching and counseling in both elementary and college settings. Ms. Strother is a counselor at Rancho Santiago Community College and an instructor at California State University, Fullerton. Her professional experience includes academic and career counseling, student teacher supervising, instructing career guidance courses, and conducting lectures on job search strategies and professional presentation skills for educators. She is a member of the California Educational Placement Association (CEPA), California Personnel Guidance Association (CPGA), California Career Guidance Association (CCGA), and Phi Delta Kappa, a professional fraternity in education.

Darrel Marshall is an administrator, with faculty rank, at the University of Arizona. His major responsibility is Educational Career and Placement Services. His graduate level education and advanced degrees are in Counseling, Education, and Higher Education Administration. Mr. Marshall's broad professional background includes over 25 years of teaching, counseling, and administration in secondary, military, and university settings. His additional experience includes counseling in the private sector, supervising student teachers, and instructing graduate courses at Chapman College, California. He is actively involved in the Association for School, College, and University Staffing (ASCUS), Rocky Mountain Educational Placement Association (RMEPA), American Association of School Personnel Administrators (AASPA), and the Association of Arizona School Administrators (ASA).

To the intelligent, talented, creative,
energetic, and faithful professionals who build our
future generations—the educators of America.

*"Whatever you can do, or dream you can, begin it.
Boldness has genius, power, and magic in it."*
—*Goethe*

Contents

Preface   ix

1   The Transition—A Career Crossroad   1
Understanding the Marketplace   2
Understanding the Employer   5
Entering the Marketplace   10
Understanding You   13
Summary   20

2   Marketing Tools—Creating Your Image with Sales Brochures   21
Your First Sales Brochure   21
Writing Your Resume   32
Introducing Yourself to the Employer   57
References   64
The Application Form   68
Summary   70

3   Searching for the Right Position—The Investment   73
Job Search Strategies   74
State Certification Information and Offices   95
Substituting   103
The Search—A Lonely Job   104
Summary   104

4   Interviewing—A Critical Task   105
Your Sales Opportunity   105
Contracts and Professional Ethics   144
Your Professional Image   147
Who Is Chosen?   148
What If I Am Not Hired?   148
Final Thoughts   150

5   Positions in Educational Administration   151
Information to Know   152
Required Professional Preparation   157
Preparing the Paperwork   159
Locating Openings   164
Understanding the Hiring Process   165
The Interview   166
Moving On and Maintaining Professionalism   168
If at First You Don't Succeed   169

6   Positions in Higher Education   171
Information to Know   171
Preparing the Paperwork   174
Locating Openings   181
Knowledge about Institutions and Positions   189
Contacting Search Committees   191
The Interview   191
Professionalism   192

7   International Positions in Education   193
Information to Know   194
Steps to Follow   201
Employment Options   203
Resources   207

Bibliography   211

Index   213

Preface

The Right Fit: An Educator's Career Handbook and Employment Guide is designed for anyone entering or changing directions in the field of education. It is a practical and complete guide for seniors and graduate students or experienced educators who are reentering, relocating, changing districts, levels, or positions in education. It will meet the needs of all educators —elementary, secondary, higher education, administration, or those seeking positions overseas.

Educators are directed and intelligent people. They know educational theory, philosophies, and principles. They understand instructional processes, methods, and techniques. Extensive internships, student teaching, and specialized training provide "hands on" practical experience. And yet, as prepared as they are in their disciplines, most are totally naive about the actual job search process. They are unsure about where to go, what to do, and how to do it. Self-confidence cultivated through years of education and experience is suddenly deflated by the thought of entering the job market or facing a hiring official. A whole different set of skills will be necessary for success in this new territory.

There are few things more important to educators than finding the position, the district, and the community which matches their personal values, goals, interests, philosophy, and life style; however, there are few who understand how to find the right career "fit."

In the near future, a shortage of educators is predicted. Everyone will be able to get a job. Maybe. Along with predicted shortages comes competition and rigid selection criteria. The purpose of this book is not simply to help you get a job. It will show you how to get the position you want, in the geographical area of your choice, the grade level and discipline you prefer. It will show you how to get the position that offers challenge and motivation—the career that produces the most favorable long-term results for you. Getting a job is now transformed into searching for your "right fit"—a meaningful personal assignment.

Candidates who get the best positions are not necessarily more qualified than you. But, they are the ones who know how to get hired. They know how to sell themselves and their strongest qualifications to the employer. Effectively using the knowledge presented in this book builds the self-confidence and skills needed to sell yourself to the employer of your choice—the one matching your needs.

National labor statistics indicate that people aged 21-35 are looking for a new position every year and a half and people over 35, every three years. Because we are a mobile population, our intent is to teach a career search process—one you will use not only now, but throughout your life. This process concentrates on the skills, knowledge, and understanding needed for a successful transition into the educator's marketplace. *The Right Fit* pulls together in a practical, step-by-step manner, tested methods that are the essential ingredients needed by educators in marketing their unique talents. It is a comprehensive, pragmatic guide, flexible enough to use in whole or part.

This handbook begins with information on the job market and how it operates, introduces you to the employer, and outlines the steps required for success. You are directed through a process of honest, personal introspection—identifying and examining what you want and what you have to offer. Complete step-by-step instructions focus your efforts on creating high-impact paperwork, developing effective job search techniques, and designing and implementing a productive plan of action. A thorough analysis of the critical interviewing stage provides information and understanding for building self-presentation skills and strengthening confidence. The final three chapters contain information specifically directed towards positions in administration, higher education, and overseas opportunities.

The Right Fit provides the insight, guidance, and encouragement to maximize your chances of gaining the position that is in harmony with your personal values, interests, and future goals. Your assignment is to effectively use this knowledge to seek and obtain the career opportunity that offers you the best possible working relationship, where you can grow professionally and personally, and where you are challenged to work at the top of your abilities.

We sincerely wish you the best in finding your professional "right fit."

CHAPTER 1

The Transition
A Career Crossroad

Transition is a time you leave one stage of your life and move toward a new desired goal.

The simple definition above implies a positive turning point—a stimulating life change of leaving the old and entering the new. Career beginnings are indeed an exciting challenge. Yet, we are also aware that the process of change begins with entering into the unknown world of job search. This transition is often associated with uncertainty, fear, and even panic.

Much of the tension and uneasiness that leads to a lack of self-confidence comes from being uninformed. Educators know achieving confidence and success begins with insight. Regardless of training, education, or professional background, new graduates and most experienced educators do not have the necessary knowledge and understanding needed for a successful transition into the marketplace.

Beginners preparing for a career in education enter a transitional stage during an internship or student teaching. Guided instruction and dedicated practice transform textbook knowledge into practical experience and move the student into the role of professional educator. Moving from campus to career is a time of personal discovery. Change and growth occur as a result of the many challenges presented by the profession.

This "learn-by-doing" experience also provides the perfect opportunity to begin expanding one's professional visibility and building a network of valuable contacts. For many, it is the first chance to have personal rapport with professional educators and get an inside look at districts, schools, and staffs. Learning what is in the job market gives the beginner a better understanding of one's career needs, and on-the-job-training is a key selling feature on resumes.

A different type of transition occurs for experienced educators seeking new positions. Some are relocating across the country or across town. Others, after an interval, want to reestablish their profession. Some may desire career changes within their current district, or may wish to take advantage of emerging opportunities in neighboring areas. A career move may be one of choice or it may be forced by changing events.

For seasoned educators, formal education is often far in the background. Professional experience is their most marketable asset. Reentering the educational career search, skilled veterans possess varied talents, training, certification, competencies, and abilities. For a successful career transition, it is important to learn how to market this valuable experience and highlight these unique qualifications to best "sell" an educator for the position that fully utilizes his or her talents and skills.

Whatever your current status: hopeful first-time applicant or experienced professional, relocating or reentering, a successful career search begins with knowledge and understanding. This first chapter provides information regarding the educator's job market, introduces you to the employer, begins the process of personal assessment, and outlines the necessary steps for a successful transition into the marketplace.

UNDERSTANDING THE MARKETPLACE

Market Analysis—Trends and Projections

GOOD NEWS FOR EDUCATORS! After experiencing more than a decade of declining enrollments, school closings, teacher layoffs, and budget restrictions, the outlook for educators is changing dramatically. Some areas of the country are already experiencing shortages of teachers because of increased birthrate and large numbers of educators retiring or leaving the field. Statisticians believe this trend will continue at the elementary and secondary levels, as well as in higher education. Projections say thirty percent or more of all professors in the United States will have to be replaced in the next eight years.

Along with the greater availability of positions, the importance of quality education is now receiving renewed public support. Positive effects are taking place: Funding levels are becoming more stable, starting salaries are increasing, teaching excellence is being recognized, and extra income is available for those identified as "mentor teachers." There is a current emphasis on raising academic standards and reducing class size. Closed campuses are reopening. Schools are being built. New legislation in some states has strengthened high school graduation requirements. Some student loans that do not have to be paid back are available for educators entering fields in which there are shortages. Because of renewed public awareness, positive legislative action, support of quality education, increased enrollment, vacancies, and new positions, this is an excellent time to be entering the educational job market. That is the good news.

The bad news, however, is that an excellent marketplace means competition for desired openings. The word is out—positions in education are once again available. Increasing numbers of students are entering and currently completing training in the field of education. College graduates from other career areas are enrolling in certification programs. Many parents, once classroom aides and volunteers, are reentry college students fulfilling degree and license requirements. Our colleges and universities across the country are experiencing a dramatic increase in interest and enrollment for programs leading to careers in education.

In addition, fierce competition for jobs comes not only from inside your state, but also from other areas of the country. Many educators are relocating with the outstanding recommendations and valuable experience new graduates lack.

Increased numbers entering the employment market prompt school districts to raise their standards and expectations. The employer is looking for the top ten percent of a graduating class; in other words, excellence is valued. With a large population of qualified applicants, districts naturally seek the most outstanding and the most motivated professionals. From this pool of "super educators," employers hire the ones who best fit their students, district, and community.

Although it is an excellent marketplace for educators, it is also a very competitive job market. Your desired position may not be easy to acquire. Success depends on your motivation to complete the job search procedure by skillfully executing the right steps at the right time. Your task of finding and obtaining the right position, the one perfect "fit" for you, is the most important task you have. *The results are well worth the effort*.

The Marketplace Schedule

The field of education has yearly cycles distinguishing it from the business world. In this country, most of our elementary and secondary institutions operate on a **semester** basis—two semesters per school year. However, there is currently a slow move toward year-round schooling. There are sixty-seven school districts in the United States using year-round school programs. (Forty-seven are located in California.) Under this plan, students attend classes for two months, then have twenty days off before returning for another two-month segment. Proponents contend year-round schedules are the only economically practical way to cope with the flood of new students into schools "already strained beyond capacity."

Another new system to ease the strain of overcrowded schools, is a **multitrack year-round** schedule. Under this program, students are divided into four groups. One group is on vacation while the other three attend classes.

Some districts include both semester-based and year-round schools. For a successful transition into the job market, it is vital to know the teaching cycle(s) of your desired areas. *The school cycle determines the school district's schedule for application, screening, and interviewing.* Your paperwork must be in the district office during defined periods of the year in order for you to be considered an applicant.

Districts on the semester cycle begin to screen and interview applicants for the spring semester (beginning in January) in mid-October. Therefore, your paperwork can be in the district office as early as October 15th. In mid-December, employers begin hiring for their spring semester's known positions. Many student teachers finishing degree and certification requirements are "too busy" to be involved in interviewing. They wait to apply in late December, and find they have missed out on the screening process. Sometimes positions may become available during the first three weeks of January for various reasons. This is a second time to try.

For the fall semester (beginning in September), districts begin to screen and interview applicants in mid-February and continue through mid-April. During that time, a few superstars may be hired for known openings. Most hiring, however, is done in May and June. For fall semester hiring, your paperwork can be in the district office as early as February 15th. Do not wait until after the semester to begin your job search. Based on enrollment, and last minute changes, applicants are sometimes hired as late as August and September, and even after school has started.

Schools on year-round and multi-track cycles may operate differently. Contact your desired districts for information regarding hiring schedules.

Remember, district schedules and timing are extremely important areas of the job search. The only way you are considered an applicant and have a chance of getting an inverview (and possibly being hired) is by getting your paperwork into the district at the right time.

UNDERSTANDING THE EMPLOYER

Who Is the Employer?

School boards have the power to hire. However, certain positions within a school district have the power to select candidates for recommendation to the board. Positions with the power to make selections vary from district to district and can be the superintendent, the personnel director, the building site principal, or even the board members themselves. When an opening exists, the most important job the employer has is to screen, interview, and select the "right" candidate. This is a crucial decision. The school district's image and reputation rest on the quality of its teachers and administrators. Hiring the "right" applicant strengthens the employer's status and respect in the district and community. (Employers need to consider their own interests.) In addition, it is a fact that when people are a good match with their working environment, they are happy, fulfilled, derive pleasure from their career, do better, stay longer, and are more productive.

Although selecting the "right" candidate is an extremely important job, the employer is not necessarily an expert at this process. Because of the stress involved, some employers feel the interviewing and selection process is the job they like the least. They may be as stressed as the applicants.

If employers make mistakes in hiring, it reflects on their reputation with the school board, the principals, the teachers, and the community. Many employers reduce some of the stress by appointing a selection committee to assist them in making the decision. However the process is accomplished, the following considerations should be applied to employers:

1. They are busy and under stress.
2. They are painfully human—bearing their own set of prejudices and interpersonal experiences.
3. They are totally consumed with one goal—finding one special human who truly fits the particular opening. And, they are greedy. They seek the cream of the crop, the superstar, the top ten percent.

Although many well-trained administrators enjoy talking with candidates and sorting from the pool, there is no doubt that employers are busy and under stress. If the district needs a teacher within the month, time becomes an additional stress factor. A quick interview, however, resulting in a "wrong" hiring, can mean loss of respect in the district and community. Too many bad judgments could cost them their jobs—not to mention high blood pressure and ulcers.

Let's observe one particular employer facing an unusually busy Monday.

The district needs another teacher—immediately. On the previous Wednesday the announced opening was posted in several university career centers. The result was 150 resumes piled on the desk. The employer has a new goal—how many of these can be removed from this desk by noon?

One by one, based on initial impressions and personal opinions, resumes are rapidly inspected and grouped into stacks of acceptable or unacceptable. There is no time to carefully read and meticulously critique each one. The employer merely skims each resume, glances briefly at some highlighted categories, makes an immediate appraisal, and sets it aside. Choosing one special person is truly a subjective activity. Personal judgment, subjective feelings, and human opinion are evaluation criteria. As the employer reads through the personal information contained in the resumes, the following impressions and thoughts may be registered:

> *Born ?* ("...hmmmmm....too young") or ("...too old.")
> *Married ?* ("No way, the last one got pregnant and left mid-year.")
> *Single ?* ("Not in my school! He'll be out every night.")
> *Kids ?* ("No, sir, she'll always be home taking care of them.")
> *No kids ?* ("What's the matter, doesn't he like children?")
> *Born in Texas ?* ("Never did like a Texan.")
> *From a small town ?* ("Last thing we need is a country bumpkin.")
> *From a big town ?* ("...won't understand or appreciate our small community.")
> *Excellent health ?* (They *all* say that!)
> *Picture ?* ("This one's not smiling, must be a cold person"), or ("Smiling too much, not serious enough for me.")

The screening process continues into the week. Based on the current submitted paperwork, combined with selections drawn from a previous pool of candidates, decisions are made. Finalists are called for an interview.

The employer begins the first interview with the question, "Tell me, Mrs. Jones, why do you want this position?" Her answer includes several facts. She is recently divorced, has three children, and has decided to return to teaching because she desperately needs a paycheck again.

Now, of course, the employer cares about human welfare, maybe more than most people. Recently this hiring official organized the local community charity fair. Both the Veteran's Hospital and the Home for Abused Children benefit from this administrator's time and effort. Although the employer cares about Mrs. Jones' personal situation, a candidate will not get the job because of those criteria.

The interviewing process continues through the week. The employer is totally consumed with one goal—find that special superstar: the individual with the outstanding abilities and qualifications that fit this single opening, in this particular district, in this specific community.

The employer is busy, human, and wants the very best, just like the rest of us.

What Do Employers Want?

This is easy. Employers want educators who are not just acceptable but are exceptional—people with the ability to take college curriculum theory and textbook methods and make them "shine" in the educator's working world. They know the key to school improvement is excellence in teaching and managing.

Remember, employers are greedy. They want nothing less than the very best, the ideal, the top ten percent. What exactly does this mean? The following is a priority list of the top ten special qualifications employers want in the perfect educator:

1. *Outstanding human skills.* Employer want someone who is well liked and who likes people. They want an educator who is loved and respected by students, parents, administrators, and coworkers. They want a charming person, one who makes every student feel special. The employer wants a person who is diplomatic. In elementary and secondary levels, the employer wants someone who is willing to work with parents and sees them as a vital part of the learning process. Employers want educators who handle problems or difficult situations with ease, maintain dignity and integrity under pressure, and radiate poise and self-confidence. The perfect educator is one who understands others, is an empathic listener, and is a caring, sharing human.

2. *Outstanding communicative skills (both oral and written).* Employers want someone who has perfect grammar, can write a flawless letter, and has excellent penmanship. They want educators who are good listeners and follow through with suggestions and directions. They want people with strong leadership abilities—consistent, yet open-minded—serious, yet not rigid. They want educators who articulate clearly and communicate in a positive and optimistic manner.

Another aspect of communication is the message one delivers through personal appearance. Employers consider *the whole package* the applicant presents. They want people who communicate a positive image of their district in appearance, style, and grooming. School districts, colleges, and universities, in general, are conservative and traditional in this respect.

3. *Motivated to teach or manage*. Employers want educators who love working with students, parents, and faculty. They want people who are eager to start the day, excited about new activities, and anxious to plan and execute innovative projects and programs. They want the special person who is always the first to arrive and the last to leave. They want someone who is willing to try new methods, is open to suggestions, and shares techniques and ideas with peers. They want a person who takes charge and makes things happen. They want the one who is motivated to teach or manage, using the ideas and concepts that match the district's administrative philosophy.

4. *Outstanding personality, character, integrity, honesty, enthusiasm, and a team player*. Employers want a person with high moral standards, and one who is physically and mentally healthy. They do not want to see one of their educator's names in the news associated with a scandal. They want people who are competent team players—supportive, cooperative, sharing, helpful—and who are valuable, active contributors. Employers want happy educators who display an eagerness and enthusiasm that is contagious.

5. *Responsible and dependable*. Employers want people who are punctual—always there on time for work, meetings, and appointments. They want someone who is reliable; someone they can depend on to complete projects and paperwork. They want an architect and an engineer—the unique person who not only designs plans, but then sets goals and gets the job done. They want someone who is organized and trustworthy.

6. *A professional in the field*. Employers want people who see themselves and their career as a profession. They want those people who have a good understanding of their field, enjoy learning and staying current in new methods, and continue building on their strengths. They seek educators who are involved in activities adding to their professional growth. This will be evident on the applicant's resume under the category "Professional Affiliations" and/or "In-service Training." Even student teachers have gone to in-services. If you do not include a professional growth area on your resume, the employer thinks you either are not involved in such activities or you do not think they are important.

7. *An actively involved community member*. Schools and educators are vital parts of the community. In small towns, the school is often the focal point of group activities. The employer wants educators who have positive visibility within their community. Remember, the employer has selfish motives. The hiring official knows that when the community feels good about the school district, more bond issues are passed. This can mean the administrators keep their jobs longer. Employers want educators who benefit them and make them

look good. It is advantageous for you to show evidence of community involvement on your resume, such as the Chamber of Commerce, Little League, Special Olympics, and Kiwanis Club. Employers only know from your resume what you tell them.

8. *Has cultural awareness.* Employers want someone with a broad background—preferably one who is familiar with other languages and who has done some world travel. Classrooms today contain students who speak various languages and who are from a multitude of backgrounds, cultures, ethnic groups, and socio-economic levels. The employer wants someone who works and relates well with all people and one who perceives and appreciates cultural differences.

9. *Has special skills.* A valuable employee takes on more responsibility than is assigned. The employer wants a person who can operate a computer, coach the after-school softball team, establish the debate league, chair a meeting, participate on the curriculum committee, organize the talent show, accompany the choral group, lead the drama club, publish the school newspaper, manage a student government group, and pull together the science fair. Educators find themselves volunteering (or being drafted) for extracurricular activities. It benefits you to show evidence of and enthusiasm for these extra projects in your paperwork and during the interview.

10. *Oh yes, employers also need someone with the right degree(s) and certification.* (Notice the priority given to this area.) Applicants who are successful in advancing to the interview stage have the right degree(s) and certification. This was determined during the paper screening process.

> *What the employer wants is the ideal: Mr. or Ms. Perfect American Educator*

Who Do Employers Hire?

MYTH: Employers hire the most qualified people they can find—the ones with the highest degrees, from the most distinguished schools, with the best grade point average, and the greatest amount of training and experience.

FACT: Employers hire people they like—individuals they feel good about; educators they feel "fit" the position. Successful applicants, those who get hired, have convinced the employer(s) that they are that perfect fit.

> *Employers hire the special person who fits their needs, their kind of district, their grade level opening or subject matter, their kind of students, parents, and their kind of community.*

A degree, straight "A's," an honor society membership, and certification, are no guarantee of placement in the position of your choice. Employers do not hire a degree, academic knowledge, a license, and a grade point average. They hire the whole person.

Interviewing is not a logical, exact science. Remember, employers use personal judgment and subjective feelings to hire the one they think is best for the position. All applicants who get an interview have the proper degree(s) and certification (or are in the process of getting them). And, in reality, many applicants may be a good "match" for the opening. Yet, employers hire *the one who makes the best overall self-presentation in making a connection with the district and its needs—the one who best demonstrates a "fitness" for that particular position.*

How do you do this? What determines success in getting hired for the position you feel matches you? The following section outlines the necessary steps for achieving your career goal.

ENTERING THE MARKETPLACE

Steps for Success

Seventy percent of your success in obtaining the right career fit is based on your marketing skills—understanding the job market and developing the ability to sell yourself. Thirty percent of your success is based on your professional skills.

Sound discouraging? By this time, most educators have invested time, effort, and money developing professional skills. Beginners have devoted several years to schooling, meeting degree and certification requirements, increasing grade point averages, studying theory, gaining knowledge, and practicing methods and skills.

Experienced educators have personal investments in mastering competencies, developing specializations, improving skills, and cultivating talents, along with obtaining advanced degrees and additional licensing. Now, we are telling you that seventy percent of your success in obtaining the right career fit has nothing to do with those areas. The fact is that *no matter how wonderful, talented, educated, creative, intelligent, and competent you are, if you can't convince the employer of it, it won't do you any good.*

Seventy percent of your success in obtaining the right career fit depends on successful completion of four important steps:

1. Have a thorough understanding of who you are and what you want. (Know your product.)
2. Develop successful sales brochures. (Create your marketing tools.)

3. Gather information on the desired position and understand the employer's special needs and wants. (Know your market.)
4. Develop the ability to sell your unique qualities that fit the position. (Practice interview presentation skills.)

To illustrate the steps for success, imagine you have taken a job in the business world as a vacuum cleaner salesperson. Your goal: To be the best, topping all others in profit and volume of sales. Now, as any good salesperson understands, the basis of all marketing is knowing the product you are selling. You need thorough knowledge of the main selling features of your machine, the various optional equipment, how it works, the length of the electrical cord, its history of dependability, ease of maintenance, size, weight, colors, and what makes your machine special.

Finding and obtaining your right career fit is based on the same principle. Your important first step for success in the educational marketplace is to study the product you are selling.

Know Your Product

Your product is you. You are selling your special combination of abilities, professional skills, talents, and future capabilities. Your sales pitch must be organized, convincing, and believable. (And it must be accomplished in thirty minutes.)

"Tell me about yourself."
   (Can you present your best qualities and abilities in an organized concise manner?)

"What grade level 'fits' you?"
   (Any grade level?—You can't convince me of that.)

"You say you have no weaknesses and had no problems in student teaching?"
   (Unbelievable.)

Self-assessment—knowing your strengths and weaknesses, knowing what you want in your professional and personal life, and having a thorough understanding of the unique qualities you offer—is the essential first step for success in the job market. Self-knowledge is not a "one shot" event. The vacuum cleaner salesperson finds that each time information is exchanged, knowledge of the product increases. Self-assessment is an ongoing, continuous process.

As the vacuum cleaner salesperson studies and gains understanding of the product, an effective advertising strategy is also planned. Time, energy, and money is spent on developing the best and most persuasive sales brochures. Special features of the machine are presented in just the right way to convince each customer this machine benefits them and meets all their needs.

In reality, there may be many vacuum cleaners that could satisfy the customer. The smart salesperson knows, however, that the key to selling is to appeal to the needs of the individual buyer. Therefore, a convincing sales-person knows there is no such thing as an "all purpose" sales brochure. Several are designed to meet the needs of many different customers. One brochure emphasizes reliability of the machine, low maintenance, and easy payment plans. Another brochure highlights designer colors, unique added features, and ease of use. These advertisements "open the door" for a possible sale.

Educators also need an effective advertising strategy to "open the door" for an interview. The second step for success in the marketplace is to spend time, energy, and money on your sales brochures.

An Educator's Marketing Tools

An applicant for a position in education has the following marketing tools or sales brochures:

Resumes or *Vitas*
College Placement/Credentials File
Business Letters
Application Forms

To develop these sales brochures into effective advertisements, you need to gather information on your buyer (the employer). You do this by studying the marketplace.

Know Your Market

The vacuum cleaner salesperson studies all aspects of the market. Who are the potential customers? What are their socio-economic levels? What are their primary concerns when buying? Where do they live? When is the best time to contact them? Why do they need my product? How do I best present and display my machine as the one that meets their needs?

Studying the educational marketplace and gathering information gives you the knowledge to revise each of your "advertisements" to fit the particular position, district, and community. Like the salesperson's brochures, there is no such thing as an all-purpose resume or business letter. An important job search skill is developing the ability to change and edit your paperwork to meet the individual employer's specific needs. Therefore, market research is a critical factor for a successful job search.

> *Every employer is different. Every employer has needs. The more you know about the employer, the better you can tailor your sales brochure to meet those needs.*

When the vacuum cleaner salesperson knows and understands the product and has designed sales brochures based on the needs of the buyer, the final and most crucial step begins. Like studying for an important final exam, time and energy is spent in thorough preparation for the sales appointment. The salesperson knows there is really only one opportunity to convince the customer to buy. Hard work, preparation, and planning are the keys to success.

The next step in your job search process is to prepare, practice, and plan for the interview.

Your Sales Opportunity

The interview is your sales opportunity. This is the time you present your best professional self in looks and demeanor. Highlight your special qualities in an enthusiastic, convincing, and believable manner. Know when to talk and when to listen, identify questions to ask, articulate concise yet comprehensive answers, and clearly communicate how your special abilities match the desired opening.

> *The most important part of your sales opportunity is presenting yourself as the professional who best fits the position and meets the needs of the employer.*

If this entire process sounds overwhelming, do not be concerned. (Serious, yes—concerned, no.) Step by step, *The Right Fit* is your guide and coach through each of these important stages. Let's begin with the first phase—an analysis of you—getting to know the product.

UNDERSTANDING YOU

Self-Assessment—Who Am I? What Do I Want?

These questions are closely related. Answering "Who am I?" is the key to understanding "What do I want?" Many experienced educators and graduate students entering the employment market respond "I know who I am and what I want. Now I just need a job." Yet, many applicants face some uncomfortable moments when confronted with interview questions such as:

"Tell me about your strengths and weaknesses."
"Where do you see yourself in five years?"
"I see all your experience is in grades 1-4; what makes you think you would be successful in a middle school?"
"Why do you want this position?"

Most people have the misconception that finding the right career means jumping into the job market. Career search, however, begins with an approach focusing on the internal you. This is a process of self-discovery—identifying your strengths and uniqueness, desires and goals, needs and wants, interests and values. The right career fit is when the total job and working environment are compatible with your inner needs and wants.

Honest introspection of your values and needs plays an important role in decision making and goal setting. With self-understanding, you can more easily define your career choice. Decisions and goals are made with a clear job search focus. You gain understanding of where you fit in your professional world. Nobody excels with every subject or grade level. Find the areas you love best, and they will also be the areas you do best.

More important than anything else, the process of self-discovery leads to feelings of acceptance and the building of a positive self-image. Remember, the product you are selling is you. You cannot convince others of your capabilities until you really believe in yourself. Strengthening your self-confidence, feeling good about who you are, and generating enthusiasm for what you have to offer are vital to succeeding in the job search process.

Work is more than earning a living. In today's world, it is an important component of your life. Work is a means of self-expression and a direct link to your ego, status, and self-esteem. How you feel about your profession and the satisfaction you gain from it to a large extent determines and influences the quality of your life. All ingredients of living—love and friendships, professional associates, leisure time and recreation, home and work environments, family life, lifestyle, and future educational and professional opportunities—are affected by your career choice. A career in education will not provide great wealth. Therefore, your "working life" must have personal benefits and offer professional enrichments.

Finding your "right fit" must be your primary goal. There is one thing worse than having no job—it is having the wrong job. Medical studies point to illnesses that are associated with remaining in unsatisfying careers. Sometimes educators stay in these situations because they do not want to give up tenure. Tenure is a false sense of security. Real inner security comes from knowing what you want, where you fit in the working world, and gaining the knowledge and necessary skills to get it.

This important inner process of career search begins a time of personal exploration and growth. Self-awareness is a dynamic, continuing process. From writing your resume to accepting or rejecting a position, every experience provides self-understanding. When entering and establishing a new career, your career is also creating a new you. Personal growth is a slow, steady process, with setbacks, detours, and obstacles along the way. Through it all, you continue to remodel yourself—transforming and progressing with new ideas, people, environments, and time.

> *Knowing who you are, where you want to go, and what you want, is an ever-changing, soul-searching, lifelong challenge.*

Written Exercises for Self-Assessment

The following self-assessment exercises are designed for guidance in understanding your special qualities, strengths, values, goals, wants, needs, interests, and desired working conditions. It is important to actually write your answers. Writing is an effective tool for self-examination. It forces you to think clearly, giving you perspective on your basic philosophies and needs.

These exercises were not intended to be practice interview questions, although many are used by employers to get a better understanding of the applicant. They are primarily designed as a tool for gathering self-information, leading to intelligent decision making and positive action. This action is your move into the educational job market, with renewed self-knowledge and confidence.

These are not easy questions, but they should prove to be revealing. For effective self-evaluation, these exercises require thought and time. Use several days or weeks to complete them. Be honest. Do not censor your answers.

> *Getting what you want begins with you:*
> *Know what you want.*
> *Know what you believe.*
> *Know what you have to offer.*
> *Know what is important to you.*

Areas of Uniqueness

1. List ten words that describe you. Rank these descriptive words in numerical order of importance, number one being the word that best describes you, and so forth.
2. List ten words describing you as an educator. Rank them in numerical order of importance.
3. How are you like other people? How are you like other educators? How are you different? Circle three words on your list that best describe how you are different.
4. Write an answer to the question: Who am I? It may include some of the following: What am I doing and what am I involved in when I feel happiest, most fulfilled, proud? In what areas of my life do I feel most confident and competent? What is the real "center" of my life? What nouns describe me? (i.e., husband, friend, mother)
5. What are your strengths and weaknesses? What are your strengths and weaknesses as an educator? Circle your top three areas of strength. How are you working to improve your weaknesses or limitations? What characteristics or areas of your life do you want to change? What weaknesses or habits have you changed with success?
6. Name the person(s) you most admire and their qualities. What fictional or historical person(s) do you most admire and why? What fictional character(s) did you most admire as a child? Looking at these people and characters, what personal qualities do you have that are similar to theirs? Circle your top three qualities.
7. List ten positive attributes you bring to the education profession. Rank them in numerical order of importance. In your experiences as an educator, what are the most important things you have learned about yourself?
8. How would your students describe you? In what ways do your students profit by having you as their teacher (or principal)? How would your coworkers and supervisors describe you?
9. What were your experiences as a student? What teachers and professors in your background influenced your decision to become an educator? What qualities do you most admire in former educators? What qualities do you most admire in educators you are currently working with or know? What qualities do you see in yourself that are similar to theirs?
10. In reviewing your responses to the above nine questions, list your five most important qualities. Next, list your five most important and meaningful qualities as an educator. What have you learned about yourself?

Areas of Value

Studies show successful people are involved in careers that are in close harmony with their most cherished values. The identification and clarification of your values actually define your career. These values are an indication of what is most important and significant in all areas of your life.

1. What is most important in your life? What do you value most? List your overall top ten values. (These may include personal values, spiritual values, lifestyle values, career values, or family values.) Rank them in the order of importance to you. How does a career in education satisfy your top three values in life?

2. Write a personal definition of the following words:

    Happiness   Success   Security   Confidence

    Circle the three words or phrases that best represent your values in each definition. How will a career in education satisfy your top three values in each definition?

3. What do you love? What do you fear? What do you worry about?

The following two exercises are difficult. Give them extra time and thought.

4. Write your philosophy of life. It may include answers to some of the following questions: What is important to you? What do you hope to accomplish in your life? What do you consider worth working for? Worth fighting for? What are you committed to? What is the purpose of your life? What are you striving for? What kind of person do you want to be? What gives your life meaning?

5. Write your philosophy of teaching or administration. It may include answers to some of the following questions: Why do you want to be an educator? (Or, why are you an educator?) When did you decide you wanted to become an educator? What significant event or time shaped your decision? What attracts you to a profession in education? What is the purpose of educating? What are your strong convictions about the field of education? What are your goals and dreams as an educator? What do you hope to accomplish in your profession? What will the profession of education do for you? What will you do for the profession of education?

6. In reviewing your philosophy of life and your philosophy of education, circle your most important values—which ones are especially significant to you? Remember that dreams, fears, goals, and purpose in life are all indicators of values. Next, review the three value questions and the philosophy questions. Make a list of your most important and

meaningful values in life. Combine personal and professional values to get a final list of ten. Then, rank them in numerical order of importance.

7. Do your values conflict? If you have a conflict of values, which one is most important to you, and would you be willing to give up or compromise on the other? How will your career as an educator satisfy these most important values in your life? What did you learn about yourself from this value exercise?

Areas of Achievement—Goals

1. What would you want to do or accomplish if you were to die in one year? Are these things a significant part of your life now?
2. What do you want written on your tombstone about your personal life and your professional life?
3. Where do you see yourself five years from now? Ten years from now?
4. What are your personal, professional, and educational goals? What are you doing toward the accomplishment of these goals?
5. What have been the biggest accomplishments in your life? What are your biggest accomplishments or achievements in the field of education? What skills were necessary for these accomplishments? What are your definitions of professional success, professional competency, professional confidence, personal success?
6. Define what it means to reach your full potential as an educator? What are you doing now in life toward achieving it? What goals have you set toward reaching it?
7. Review your most important goals, desires and dreams. How will a career in education help you achieve these goals?

Areas of Needs, Wants, and Interests

1. Is there life after school? Write your personal interests, hobbies, or passions outside of work. What special skills do these require? How are these affected by your career choice?
2. What are your special needs and wants? These include physical needs (sports, exercise, health, diet, appearance, climate), intellectual needs (research, areas of study, educational goals), creative needs (writing, composing, music, art, decorating, gardening), interpersonal needs (friendships, love, family, social events and concerns), spiritual needs (religion, church, spiritual well-being). These also include recreational and hobby needs, need for status, money, emotional well-being, needs

for success and self-confidence, home, privacy, creativity.

3. Review your needs, wants, and interests. How are these affected by your career choice? Will a career in education meet these areas of needs and interests?

Areas of Environmental Needs and Working Conditions

1. What kind of community meets your ideal living environment and working environment? Do you need a large or small town, midwest rural or large city? Is it important to be near the theater, university, cultural events, beach, mountains, or desert? Would you be happy working and living in a small town? Would you want to work in the same town where you live? List the advantages and disadvantages of each situation. How do the other people and aspects of your life play a part in these decisions?

2. How far are you willing to commute to work? (One student thought she would be willing to drive an hour each morning and evening on crowded freeways for the job she desired. After a practice run for one week, she declined the job offer.)

3. Are you willing to relocate to get the position you want? How will this affect the other aspects of your life?

4. What type of students do you prefer to work with—high or low socio-economic level, high or low achievers, multicultural, bilingual? Why? Would you prefer students from rural or urban communities? (The community reflects the type of students it has.) Do you want to work in a school with very strong parent involvement and participation? Why or why not? List the advantages or disadvantages.

5. What is your ideal teaching (or administrating) situation—self-contained classrooms, open classrooms, individualized approach, team teaching? If you do not know, then visit these different types of environments. (A student teacher commented he was glad to have had the opportunity to teach in an open-classroom situation, because now he knows he would never accept a position in one. Yet, others love it.) Find out what you want.

6. What grade level(s) or subject(s) do you prefer? What experience or knowledge influences your decision? Would you be willing to work in other areas? If you have no experience in the area, what makes you think you would succeed?

7. What salary and benefits do you feel you must have in your contract? (Each district has a different salary and benefit package.) What other working and living conditions and environments are important to you?

Evaluation

On a separate sheet of paper make a summary evaluation. This is an outline listing your five special characteristics and strengths; top five values, primary goals, and dreams; significant areas of needs, wants, and interests; and desired working conditions.

This summary sheet identifies your personal and professional priorities and your special abilities and qualities: Who you are and what you want from from career, from your education, from your life. This evaluation is the beginning of self-knowledge.

SUMMARY

A successful career search begins with knowledge and understanding. This chapter examined important external knowledge—the educator's job market, the employer, and the necessary steps for a successful transition into the marketplace. In addition, the importance of internal knowledge and understanding has been highlighted, and a self-assessment questionnaire has been completed.

The next step is to translate your self-assessment evaluation into the context of the employer's wants and needs. In other words, how are your special assets relevant to the potential employer's needs, and how do you best sell your unique qualities? Chapter 2 provides a step-by-step process for putting your special qualities into your sales brochures.

CHA2TER

Marketing Tools
Creating Your Image with Sales Brochures

Educators have four essential marketing tools: resumes or *vitas*, cover letters, college placement (or credentials) files, and application forms. This paperwork is the bridge connecting you with a potential employer. Each completed document, representing your professional image, becomes your sales brochure. Together, they play a decisive role in the screening and application process and can lead the way to the job interview.

> *If your paperwork is poorly done, you will be eliminated from the competition and will not reach the interview stage.*

As a serious applicant in a highly competitive job market, it is essential to have a thorough understanding of the application process. You need to understand the function and significance of your marketing tools and how they influence your success. It is important to develop each sales brochure as a clear and convincing picture of your best qualities. It is necessary to devote time, thought, and effort to this important task. This chapter is designed to help you prepare the paperwork that serves as your marketing tools in the screening and application process.

YOUR FIRST SALES BROCHURE

At one time a position in education could be obtained by having an inside contact or a recommendation. A telephone call or meeting with the administrator at the right time secured the job. Resumes were usually not a significant part of the process. In today's competitive job market, it is a different story.

Public education, a governmental process, is subject to strict employment guidelines. Among other things, it has felt the impact and increasing significance of Equal Opportunity and Affirmative Action legislation. Our educational institutions are required to publicize openings. One new advertised vacancy could result in hundreds of responses. Each year applicants face fierce competition for desirable positions, while employers deal with strict hiring policies and procedures in screening the increasing number of qualified candidates.

To evaluate all applicants in an efficient and impartial manner, school districts find it necessary to place new emphasis on the preliminary screening process. Currently, a commonly required first step is to have candidates submit a professional resume (or *vita*—see chapter 6, "Positions in Higher Education.")

Do not minimize the importance of this first sales brochure. Of all required paperwork, it is currently the most decisive factor in whether or not you get an interview. It is also the foundation for completing all other documents.

Give high priority to the task of rewriting and editing your resume. Positive results are in direct proportion to your committed effort. Spending time and energy developing an advertisement, which creates a favorable first impression and sells you as the right fit for the opening, could be the best investment you ever make. Quality, high-impact, persuasive resumes result in more interviews. This increases your chances of getting the interview(s) you most desire. Regardless of how you find out about openings, having a convincing, effective resume that creates positive attention and interest is an essential ingredient for success in the marketplace.

What Is a Resume?

A resume is a written, personalized statement briefly summarizing your special combination of skills, academic background, training, and professional experience—written in a manner that reflects your qualifications for a particular position. If that sounds difficult, let's put it this way: a resume is your self-assessment, tailored to the employer's needs, written in an organized outline.

A convincing, persuasive resume is a document directed to a specific employer that clearly communicates three things:

1. Your abilities and capabilities, accompanied by your accomplishments and results—not just what you do, but how well do you do it.
2. Your personal qualities and professional image—creating a picture of you as a special human being and a true professional.
3. How you "fit" the position—focusing attention on the qualifications

that meet the employer's needs and match that particular position, district, and community.

What a Resume Will and Will Not Do for You

Although your persuasive sales brochure perfectly meets the employer's needs, by itself it will not get you your desired position. Applicants are not hired on the basis of a resume alone.

This first document is the bait. Hoping to hook the employer, you present your value, capabilities, and potential contributions in an interesting, appealing way, capturing attention and curiosity. The purpose of the resume, therefore, is to entice employers, motivating them to invite you for an interview —thus opening the door for the sales meeting. A convincing, persuasive marketing tool is beneficial to you in many ways:

- It can be sent to prospective employers or be left with contacts when you are gathering information. It can be given to a person who knows someone in need of an educator with your qualifications.
- It can be used as a source of information for writing cover letters and completing application forms.
- It helps you get valuable interviews. By altering and tailoring your resume, you highlight specific qualifications that relate directly to the particular position(s) you desire.
- It can be referred to in an interview, bringing to attention your strongest qualifications and "fitness" for the position.
- It tells the employer how you get the job done. It is a demonstration of your thoroughness, accuracy, organizational skills, and written communication abilities.
- It gives the employer an understanding of how you see yourself as a professional educator and as an individual.
- By aiming your resume efforts in the direction of the positions that best fit you, it can be the step leading to immediate career satisfaction with greater long-term results.
- It helps clarify your personal and professional goals, giving you a stronger sense of career direction.

It is possible you could get an interview without a resume. However, most of the time, you will need one to start the paperwork process. A word of caution: It is best not to use one of the many resume services listed in the yellow pages. Although a few may custom design resumes to meet employers' needs, most do not. Employers are quick to spot assembly line resumes. They feel these applicants lack initiative, self-confidence, discipline, and/or sufficient interest to write their own resumes.

If needed, attend a resume-writing workshop for guidance and motivation, ask advice from counselors and educators, have someone proofread your document for clarity and grammar, and/or use a professional typing and printing service. But basically, *write your resume yourself*. Furthermore, putting yourself through the discipline of preparing a resume is an extremely valuable exercise. You bring into focus your strongest qualifications and abilities that fit the position. This process mentally prepares you for the interview. *Competent knowledge of the product makes a more confident salesperson.*

When the task of resume preparation is undertaken conscientiously and seriously, it becomes part of your personal contract in finding your professional "right fit."

Basic Resume Guidelines

As an individual, you have special interests, personal values, future ambitions, and unique qualifications. Your first sales brochure is a reflection of your professional style and personality—each one as individual as a thumbprint.

The best part about resume preparation is that you, the author, are in full control. This is not true about other parts of the job search. You have no power over locations and availability of openings, who is interviewing candidates, questions asked in the screening and interviewing process, or qualifications of the many other applicants. Your resume and accompanying cover letter are the one area in the job search over which you have full command. And if these are poorly done, it is self-defeating.

Having full control means you plan, organize, and design it. There is no one magic formula, secret of success, or select model that works for everyone. You may not believe it by looking at job search books, but there really is no official regulation declaring a guaranteed right way to prepare a resume. Nor is there a federal law stating all resumes must be either chronological, functional, or targeted. Many people look upon this document as a "square filling" exercise. Students ask for a resume form. In essence, they are saying, "Tell me what to write and where to write it."

Resumes do include much of the same standard information. However, as a unique individual:

- YOU carefully select what information to include (and what to leave out) to present and promote the professional image you wish to convey.
- YOU organize categories, focusing attention on your unique competencies and qualities.

- YOU determine the arrangement and sequence of material to best high-light your particular "fitness" for the position.

To facilitate resume preparation, assistance is offered in the form of suggestions, guidelines, and recommendations. Examples are provided for support and motivation. This book, however, does not provide any standard resume form, model, or style.

We invite you to think of resume writing as an opportunity to launch your sales campaign by personally designing your own convincing, dynamic, persuasive advertisement. By presenting just enough information in just the right way, you draw a picture of yourself. This professional self-portrait tells the employer what you want them to know.

Before anyone gets carried away with thoughts of designing a witty, amusing, or highly unusual sales brochure, applicants also need to acknowledge and accept that school districts are conservative and traditional, and they hire professional, businesslike people. Therefore, although the composition and orchestration of this theme is in your hands, forget flamboyant designs, brightly colored paper, fancy binders, novel gimmicks, cute jargon, flashy embellishments, and elaborate type settings. These may indeed attract attention, but it may not be the kind of attention you want.

Using your own professional style, provide clear, straight-forward, organized information, in a concise, simplified, businesslike manner. With this important advice in mind, here are ten basic guidelines to keep your creative ideas within the conservative educator's professional world:

1. *A resume is a concise outline.* It is not a biographical essay. It does not contain a comprehensive list of every job you have ever had. Nor does it include a detailed history of your life or family. Your sales brochure illustrates your communication abilities in selecting and presenting a clear, concise outline of who you are and what you can do for the position.
2. *Make it brief.* Because of the number of resumes submitted for each opening, employers skim them quickly (ten to forty seconds per resume). If your document is too long, it will not be considered; therefore, one page is recommended (definitely one page for beginning educators). With several degrees, considerable experience, a variety of publications, and numerous honors and credits to your name, a longer resume is acceptable.
3. *Set high standards when it comes to typing and printing.* The business world uses quality typewriters, quality computer printers, and black ink. Buy a new typewriter ribbon for your final copy or consider having

it professionally reproduced. Use twenty pound (or slightly heavier) 8½″ x 11″ white, off-white, or beige-tinted paper. Presenting a professional-looking document communicates respect for your work, for yourself, and for the district to which you are applying.

4. *This business correspondence must be letter perfect.* Do not waste your time preparing one unless the final product is neat, organized, uncluttered, free of typographical errors, visually attractive, and has perfect spelling, punctuation, and grammar.

5. *A professional-looking layout, structure, and arrangement of information requires careful thought.* You control how the reader sees you by the way you format material. You can force the eyes to certain priority areas with the use of centered headings, underlining, capitals, and double spacing to clearly identify categories. As an employer skims a resume, the eyes focus on certain information and the mind registers brief impressions. This outline forms an image of you, the applicant.

6. *This is your advertisement.* Therefore, put your strongest statements at the top, accompanied by an at-a-glance overview of your best qualifications. A positive first impression means your resume is considered (or actually read) again. Every sales brochure has a general tone and feeling. Design one that is professionally dignified, accomplishment-oriented, and interesting.

7. *Leave ample margin space.* Employers many times use it for notes. Do not cram your document with too much material. At the same time, structure it to fill the page by introducing white space at the top and bottom and between paragraphs.

8. *A persuasive resume is clear, concrete, and to the point.* Nearly all material will be written in brief, direct statements, instead of complete sentences. (It is perfectly fine, however, to incorporate a few carefully chosen sentences, as you will see in the examples.) Use action words to create high-impact phrases. Every carefully chosen word and statement must promote you. Avoid the pronoun I, and monotonous repetition. Use short paragraphs. Valuable, relevant information must be presented quickly, concisely, and be easy to read and follow.

9. *Be factual and 100 percent honest.* Do not exaggerate or brag. Do, however, emphasize and highlight your best qualities. Leave out anything that could be used against you or make you non-marketable. Do not include your age, place of birth, photo, marital status, height, weight, religion, political affiliation, number of children, or any other personal or irrelevant information. Every thought must be directly related to your professional goal. Get to the point and stick to it. Do not let the

reader's thoughts wander from the overall professional picture you are presenting.

10. *Aim your resume in the direction of the specific target you are seeking.* This is done by focusing attention on your strongest abilities that meet the employer's needs. Consequently, *you need more than one resume.* As with anything, the first one demands the greatest amount of time and effort. From then on, tailor data to feature your most marketable qualities that fit the particular position.

Using Action Words to Show Accomplishment

Instructing a class
Managing a staff meeting
Conducting parent-teacher conferences
Solving conflicts
Supervising a committee
Counseling students
Chairing a committee
Coaching a team
Evaluating a faculty

A mental picture of the tasks listed above depicts active, busy human beings, using speech, listening skills, and body language for effective communication. Involved in these activities, educators are advising or informing, conveying a message, expressing an intent or purpose, or making a point. It is amazing how these same dynamic, active individuals produce dull, boring resumes. Your most important sales brochure must create a *word picture* of you as an alert, vibrant, professional. To create this high-impact word picture, *use action words and statements to show what you accomplish, what problems you solve, and what results take place when you are in charge.*

Eliminate overused phrases such as, "I was responsible for...," and "my duties included...." These statements do not describe beneficial results or successful achievements. Nor do they paint a picture of you as a special human being. (What educator does not have responsibilities and duties?) These unnecessary, out-dated, passive clichés take up valuable space.

> *Replace passive clichés with action words and phrases stating specific examples of how your strong qualifications lead to significant results.*

Employers are looking for people with potential. Be forceful and direct in showing what you contribute. In designing your accomplishment-oriented sales brochure, ask yourself the following:

- When totally involved and working at the peak of my abilities, what are the positive outcomes and results?
- What goals and objectives are achieved because of my special talents and qualifications?
- What specific things do I accomplish that add to, improve, or change the situation for the better?

It is not an easy task to describe accomplishments in a direct and concise outline. A lesson can be learned from the business world. Commercial enterprises deal with concrete numbers, percentages, and dollar figures to express results:

"Reduced costs 7 percent."
"Increased production by 50 percent in one year."
"Exceeded the quota by 21 percent."

As accountable educators, we also deal with real numbers on a regular basis. When possible, state them to make an impact. Compare these two statements:

"Incorporated learning centers into math program."
"Incorporated math learning centers—increased test scores 40 percent."

Without exact figures, *estimate* to the best of your knowledge. (Be able to explain in the interview, if necessary, how you arrived at the figures.) The words *significantly* and *substantially* can also be used.

"Incorporated math learning centers—increased test scores significantly."

Each time you present an accomplishment, you communicate what happened as a result of your special abilities. You make a powerful impact as an active, dynamic professional. Compare the sales difference in the following two examples:

EDUCATOR—1981 to present. Grades 4-6. My duties included teaching math, reading, language, social studies, science, art, physical education, and music. I conducted parent conferences, tested and evaluated students, and participated in open house and Back-To-School Night. I planned field trips. My extracurricular activities included setting up the after-school sports program and adding new science activities.

EDUCATOR—1981 to present. Grades 4-6. Implemented hands-on science program, culminating in five blue ribbons at the district Science Fair. Designed tests to target student needs. Developed instructional language activity centers to solve specific learning problems, increasing test scores 23 percent! Supervised extracurricular sports activities. Parents' participation in final games brought enthusiastic response and increased rapport.

The first example explains the standard basic duties of an elementary educator. The second example transforms those passive duties into active accomplishments and achievements. Omitting unnecessary words (I, and, the, my), it presents a concise picture of an involved professional. Using basically the same amount of space, the total impact is far more effective.

Incorporating action words and statements into your resume is a key requirement for a successful sales brochure. Table 1 gives you some ideas with a partial list of action words. Table 2 illustrates how to use action words to create high-impact statements with accomplishment-oriented results.

Table 1.
Action Words

accomplish	direct	integrate	question
achieve	discipline	interface	realize
acted as	discover	interpret	receive
active in	display	interview	recognize
adapt	distribute	introduce	recommend
administer	document	judge	redesign
advise	draft	lead	refer
allocate	earn	lecture	reinforce
analyze	edit	locate	relate
anticipate	eliminate	maintain	reorganize
approve	employ	manage	report
arrange	enact	mediate	represent
assess	encourage	modify	research
assign	enforce	monitor	resolve
assist	enhance	motivate	review
attend	establish	negotiate	revise
balance	estimate	observe	schedule
budget	evaluate	obtain	screen

(continued)

Table 1.
Action Words *(continued)*

calculate	examine	operate	select
clarify	expand	order	set up
coach	explain	organize	simplify
communicate	express	originate	solve
compare	facilitate	oversee	speak
complete	follow up	participate	standardize
conduct	formulate	perceive	stimulate
consult	gain	perform	strengthen
control	generate	persuade	structure
cooperate	guide	pinpoint	substitute
coordinate	handle	plan	summarize
counsel	identify	predict	supervise
create	illustrate	prepare	support
culminate in	implement	prescribe	teach
decide	improve	present	test
define	improvise	prevent	train
delegate	increase	produce	transform
demonstrate	influence	promote	translate
design	inform	propose	treat
determine	initiate	prove	utilize
develop	inspect	provide	verify
devise	inspire	publicize	win
diagnose	instruct	publish	write

Table 2.
Action Statements with Accomplishment-Oriented Results

This chart demonstrates using action words to create an accomplishment-oriented word picture. Basic duties and responsibilities are described in the first column. The second column changes these passive phrases into active statements. The third column includes accomplishment-oriented results. Adding results lengthens paragraphs. Selectively choose those that best market you for your desired position.

PASSIVE	ACTIVE	ACTIVE: WITH ACCOM-PLISHMENT-ORIENTED RESULTS
Responsible for teaching low math group.	Designed and implemented math activity centers and cooperative group activities for slow learners.	Motivated slow learners by implementing math activity centers and cooperative learning groups—increased test scores 40 percent.

Table 2.
Actions Statements with Accomplishment-Oriented Results *(continued)*

PASSIVE	ACTIVE	ACTIVE: WITH ACCOMPLISHMENT-ORIENTED RESULTS
Duties included working with gifted students.	Organized and initiated individualized language program for gifted students.	Organized and initiated individualized language program for gifted students, culminating in successful book publishing project.
Duties included planning team teaching.	Coordinated team teaching activities.	Coordinated team teaching activities resulting in increased understanding and cooperation among all primary grades.
Responsibilities included working with students of different cultures.	Designed 11th grade values unit for multicultural student population.	Designed 11th grade values unit, resulting in improved understanding among multicultural student populations.
Duties included helping master teacher in senior debate club.	Played important role in supervising senior debate club.	Played important role in supervising senior debate club. Students' enthusiasm and parents' positive response exciting.
Duties included working with tennis team after school.	Managed and directed after-school tennis team, involving thirty seniors.	Strengthened tennis team by managing and directing after-school practice for thirty seniors, resulting in second place district championship.
Enjoy teaching art lessons.	Prepared and displayed creative art activities.	Prepared creative art activities, increasing students' interest and abilities. District art show awarded four blue ribbons.
Worked with behavior problems.	Set fair consistent limits combined with positive warm support.	Strengthened self-discipline and created optimal learning environment by setting fair consistent limits combined with positive support.

(continued)

Table 2.
Actions Statements with Accomplishment-Oriented Results *(continued)*

PASSIVE	ACTIVE	ACTIVE: WITH ACCOM-PLISHMENT-ORIENTED RESULTS
As assistant principle—in charge of attendance, discipline, and class scheduling.	Scheduled classes. Initiated student management groups to boost morale, attendance, and discipline.	Scheduled classes. Initiated student management groups to boost morale, attendance, and discipline. Results—fantastic! Students' input built positive communication and school spirit.
Responsibilities included teaching anthropology to college freshmen.	Organized series of cooperative learning groups. Each presented different survival techniques of early man.	Perfect attendance and high interest when cooperative learning groups presented survival techniques of early man. Significant improvement in test scores.
Responsibilities included handling college drama activities.	Planned, organized, and directed drama programs for 1500–student college.	Planned, organized, and directed drama programs for 1500–student college; increased number of productions by 25 percent.
I talked with parents about student's individual needs.	Actively involved parents in students' individualized learning contracts.	Actively involved parents in students' individualized learning contracts. Improved skill mastery and increased parent/student/teacher communication.

WRITING YOUR RESUME

With an understanding of basic resume guidelines and use of action words for accomplishment-oriented results, the next step is the actual writing of your document.

The following is a list of major categories to be included in a professional educator's resume:

Identification
Professional Objective
Certification
Education
Professional Experience (includes student teaching, internships,
     practicums, volunteer, part–time, assistantships, research, and
     consulting)
Placement/Credentials File (Number and location)

The following is a list of optional categories. Some or all could be included, if appropriate:

Professional Affiliations and Activities (includes association member-
     ships, conferences, in-services, publications, and other profes-
     sional involvement)
Community and College Activities
Awards, Honors, and Grants
Special Skills, Language Competencies, Interests, Hobbies, Talents,
     and Travel
Military Service

Identification

Your legal or professional name centered at the top of the page becomes the title of your sales brochure. Type your name the same way on all documents for each employer. Do not include Mr., Mrs., Miss, Ms., Junior, Senior, surname numbers (II), nicknames, or a company title. If you hold a doctorate, you may add it after your name.

If your resume is longer than one page, put your name on each page. On the first page, follow your name with your complete mailing address and zip code. Avoid abbreviations. Spell out all parts of the address. Include a permanent forwarding address if you are in the process of moving or living in a dormitory.

Always include a telephone number and area code. If you do not have an answering machine and are seldom home during work hours, ask (or hire) someone to handle your calls during your job search. Then state a permanent number and a message number on your document. Do not use category titles, such as name, telephone, resume. This is self-evident information.

There are many ways to present your identification. Here are three examples:

Lorran E. Watson
8768 Hillside Drive, Clifford, Nevada 55000
Home: (600) 987-6543   Message: (600) 123-4321

Lorran E. Watson

Permanent:	Dormitory:
8768 Hillside Drive	765 Parkside Lane
Clifford, Nevada 55000	Millville, Nevada 55000
(600) 987-6543	(601) 789-6576

Lorran E. Watson

8768 Hillside Drive   (600) 987-6543   Clifford, Nevada 55000

Professional Objective

The professional objective is the theme of your resume. It serves an important and specific function. As the heart and focus of your sales brochure, all other material, details, information, and facts, relate to and support this theme.

Your objective requires special thought, since stating it in just the right way is critically important in developing a successful marketing tool. After your personal identification, the professional objective is the first category noticed by the employer. As in any good advertisement, the high-impact sales message is at the top of the page. If you do not hook the buyer in your first few lines, your resume may not receive any further consideration.

The professional objective has two main functions. One is to clearly identify the position and level you desire. Employers want people who know who they are and what they want. You will not convince a hiring official you are terrific at every grade level. But, how is it possible to state a grade level preference without limiting one's possibilities? You do this by including a *want to statement* (what you prefer to do), and a *willing to statement* (what you are capable of doing). Compare the two examples:

Will take any teaching position in grades 7–12.

Secondary Math Educator—preference for senior high, but willing
    to teach at middle school level.

Notice how the second example clearly identifies a preference (want to) statement, without limiting the possibilities (by adding the willing to statement). The following are more examples of want to and willing to statements:

Elementary Educator—prefer grades 1–4, but willing to teach other levels.

Desire position as **Junior High School Principal**, but willing to work with elementary grades.

Desire position as a **Tenure-Track Professor**—preference for graduates, but willing to work with undergraduates.

The second function of the professional objective is to generate positive interest and attention, and to create a favorable first impression. You do this by enhancing your want to and willing to statements with a description of your highest qualifications, interests, or skills that best sell you for the position you desire.

The following objective was written by an applicant seeking a position in a multicultural, bilingual area. There were several openings in this district, mostly at the K-4 grade level.

PROFESSIONAL OBJECTIVE
Elementary Educator—preference for grades K-4, but willing to teach upper levels—interested in working with multicultural, bilingual student population; where there is a need for incorporating reading and language activity centers, encouraging parental involvement, and increasing multicultural appreciation through character building programs.

The same applicant applied in another district. This time the exact opening was known—a second grade teaching position. The school is located in an upper socio-economic level neighborhood. Knowing this, the specific position was stated in the objective, and different qualifications were highlighted:

PROFESSIONAL OBJECTIVE
Second Grade Elementary Educator—where there is a need for an individualized language and math approach—incorporating art, dramatics, and music into the curriculum—excellent interpersonal skills in generating parent involvement and motivating each student to achieve success and develop individual talents.

The more you tailor or fine tune your objective to specifically fit the district or position, the better. If you obtain a printed job description, use it to write your professional objective to perfectly match the opening. Do not misunderstand. We are not saying make up (or lie) in order to write an objective to fit the job. The remaining information in your resume (and, of course, your interview presentation) must prove everything you say in your first paragraph. What we are emphasizing is that *based on your past experience and future potential, design your professional objective to highlight your strongest qualifications that best meet the employer's needs.*

A high-impact sales approach emphasizes that you have exactly what the buyer wants. By stating your desired position and highest qualifications at the top of your sales brochure, you are immediately telling the employer, "This is what I have to offer." By the way, never mention what the employer can offer you, as in the following example:

> Looking for any teaching position with a district that offers the opportunities for beginning my master's degree training towards my future goal as an administrator.

The applicant makes it very clear what is desired from the employer, yet provides no indication of what is being offered. Another mistake made in the example is stating long-term goals. People sometimes think this makes them appear ambitious. Instead, employers conclude the position is interesting to the applicant only because it can lead to future goals. (Employers reading this objective may think the applicant is going after their job.) Your objective should reflect only your immediate career choice, showing what you now offer. To paraphrase John F. Kennedy's inaugural message, "Think not what the position can do for you—but what you can do for the position."

To summarize suggestions for writing your professional objective:

1. Use a *want to statement* and a *willing to statement* to identify your desired level and position. (Or write your objective to fit one specific opening.)
2. Capture attention by highlighting your strongest qualifications that match the employer's needs.
3. Show what you can do for the employers, not what they can do for you.

The following are additional examples of professional objectives:

PROFESSIONAL OBJECTIVE
Position as a **Tenure-Track History Professor**—anxious to work with both undergraduates and graduates, where real life experiences of

living and teaching three years in Europe and Japan will be utilized to full advantage.

PROFESSIONAL OBJECTIVE
Secondary Level Drama Instructor—preference for high school, but willing to teach junior high where there is a need for creative progressive drama programs and high energy directing of individual and group activities that inspire cooperative effort and skill improvement. Anxious and willing to sponsor extended-day drama activities.

PROFESSIONAL OBJECTIVE
Assistant Principal—elementary level preferred, but willing to work at middle school where there is a need for strong consistent supervision and guidance, goal setting and evaluation, effective problem-solving programs, and increased rapport between faculty, parents, and students.

As the theme of your sales brochure, your professional objective states your case. Now your job is to supply the evidence that supports your claim.

The purpose of the remaining categories, the body of your resume, is to highlight clearly your qualifications that *confirm, prove, and give validity to your objective*. Minimize or omit all other information. In other words, as you tailored your professional objective to fit the position, now tailor the information in the body of your resume to match your objective.

Certification

Clearly state your certification [also referred to as one's license(s) or credential(s)], so employers immediately see what areas and levels you are licensed to instruct or manage. We suggest you include this information immediately following your professional objective. Out-of-state applicants must show evidence they either have the necessary license or are moving toward certification. (You can use the words "pending," "applied for," or "in progress.")

For applicants currently completing certification requirements within the marketplace time frame, simply state your certification followed by the month and year. (In other words, even if the date has not yet occurred, it is not necessary to use "expected" if completion is within the next few months.)

Include only certification that supports your objective. If you are applying for a position as a college instructor, do not include an elementary teaching certification, unless, of course, you plan to teach future elementary educators. An exception to this guideline concerns administrative candidates. It is important for administrators to show a logical career progression by stating all certification, from teaching through administration. (See chapter 5, "Positions in Educational Administration.")

Present your most recent certification first, or, list the license first that best matches your professional objective. An example is an applicant with a teaching credential (received 1985) and a counseling certification (received 1989). If applying for a teaching position (with the possibility of limited counseling duties), then state the teaching certification first, because teaching is the advertised position and therefore the applicant's main objective. The following are examples of certification presentation:

CERTIFICATION
Reading Specialist Credential, Arizona, May 1990.
Multiple Subjects Credential, California, 1986.

CERTIFICATION
Utah Secondary Teaching Credential, Science, in process.
Single Subject Credential, Science, Oregon, 1987.

CERTIFICATION
Texas State Standard Superintendents Certificate, granted 1989.
Texas Secondary Principal Certificate, granted 1986.
Texas Standard Secondary Teaching Certificate, English, 1983.

Education

Like certification, clearly state your education so the employer sees at a glance you either have the necessary degree(s), or it is in progress. New graduates should position the education category directly after certification, since it is an important qualification, and professional experience is limited. With a background of several years in the field, you may choose to place education after experience.

In the education category, indicate your degree and where you received it. Follow with the year it was or will be acquired. (Again, for students receiving degrees within the marketplace time frame, simply state the degree, followed by the month and year—even though the date has not yet occurred.) Include majors, minors, honors, high grade point average, scholarships, and relevant coursework, as appropriate.

It is best to limit the amount of schools to three. Omit a two-year, Associate of Arts degree, unless you received awards or special honors. Omit all reference to high school. Enrollment in a fifth-year graduate teaching program can be stated Graduate Studies or Post Baccalaureate Teacher's Certification Program.

Begin with your highest level of education, or, like certification, state the education that best matches your objective. For example, an applicant has two graduate level degrees. The first degree presented should be the one that best fits the job description, regardless of when it was obtained. If you choose to state your grade point average (G.P.A.), do so only if it is above 3.0.

If your academic institution is well known, has the state's name in the college title, and/or you are applying for positions in the same area as your university or college, it is not necessary to include the name of the state in which the college is located.

Examples

The following applicant's career goal is elementary education. The Early Childhood Education major and Psychology minor clearly supports the objective and is therefore appropriate for highlighting:

ACADEMIC STUDIES
Bachelor of Arts Degree, Northern State University, May 1990.
> Early Childhood Education major, Psychology minor. 12 units completed in special education. Studies financed by summer and part-time employment in Walter Pre-School, Newwood.

The applicant included how school expenses were financed. Employers like people who work in the real world while pursuing their education. If you did so, state it here or in your cover letter. Add where you worked only if it supports your objective.

The following example demonstrates how an applicant handled an out-of-date degree. The bachelor's degree was received in 1965 from a college outside his application area (therefore, the state is included). He recently returned to a local college to complete certification requirements. Feeling the 1965 date was nonmarketable information, the applicant decided to omit it. (You may be required to report your date of graduation on an application form. With your resume, however, YOU are in control.)

PROFESSIONAL PREPARATION
Postbaccalaureate Teacher's Certification Program, Western State University, 1988-1989. All "A's" in graduate courses.
Bachelor of Arts Degree, Cordova College, Wisconsin. English Major.
> President of Student Council. Freshman English tutor, senior year.

The following applicant received a bachelor's degree in business, then returned to school to complete elementary teaching certification requirements. Feeling the business degree was nonmarketable data, the applicant chose to omit it and instead included a reason for entering the education field.

EDUCATION

Graduate Studies—Teacher's Certification Program, Calvert College, 1988-1989. Special emphasis on developing learning centers, cooperative group activities, and building self-esteem along with academics.

Bachelor of Arts Degree, Hart University, 1987. Student Council. Last year college expenses financed by part-time employment in Almont Elementary School District—sparked strong interest in the profession of education.

The following example demonstrates how to include incomplete graduate studies. The Associate of Arts degree was added because of the teaching-related activity and the scholarship. This student was a foreign exchange student in high school, and chose to add that information to the professional studies section.

PROFESSIONAL STUDIES

Graduate Studies, Sunland College, 1988-1989, 15 credits toward Master's Degree, Biology.

Bachelor of Science Degree, Central State University, 1987, Biology. President of Science Club. Biological Institute of America, student assistant, 1986-87.

Associate of Arts Degree, Baker Community College, 1985. Chapman Scholarship Award. Lab assistant, Riverside High School Biology department, 1986. Foreign exchange student, Japan, 1982.

If you choose to include a thesis or dissertation in the education category, begin the information on a new line (as the following applicant did), or list it separately under Publications and Presentations.

ACADEMIC STUDIES

Ph.D., Southern Country University, Education Administration, expected 1992.

Doctorate Dissertation in progress: "Public Relations—A New Image
for Schools"
Scholarship award—Phi Beta Gamma.

Master of Arts Degree, Lowlands College, Idaho, 1986, Education.
Master's Thesis: "Future Perspectives in Administrative Policies: A
Democratic Approach to Leadership"—published, *Journal of
Education*, vol. 6, June 1986.

Bachelor of Arts Degree, Cum Laude, Lowlands College, Idaho, 1981,
Liberal Arts, Dean's list three years.

Professional Experience

Include all areas of professional experience that directly relates to and supports
your objective. Omit all other work-related history. If you have no paid experience as an educator, show you have made the most of the opportunities you
have had. Highlight your successful performances and emphasize your strong
potential. This category includes volunteer and part-time work, as well as
student teaching, practicums, internships, field work, substituting, research,
consulting, and teaching assistantships.

Identify the position, location, and dates, beginning with the most marketable experience, not necessarily the most current one. In other words, in
presenting your first working-world self-portrait, use the professional experience that best promotes and proves your professional objective.

For each position, clearly state what you did and how well you did it.
Stress your successes. This category clearly demonstrates the value of using
action words to show accomplishment-oriented results. Never add self-apprai-
sal, such as "If it hadn't been for me, my coworkers would have never made
it through the semester.") But you may choose to include brief statements of
oral or written praise.

Examples

The following applicant chose to include a ten-year period of unrelated work
experience, tailoring it to fit the professional objective. Normally, do not justify
in a resume or cover letter why you left a position (although be prepared to
explain why in an interview). In this case, the reason for leaving supports the
objective.

PROFESSIONAL EXPERIENCE

Special Education Instructor—Student teacher, Carrington, 1989. Self-contained classroom, eighteen educationally handicapped students. Developed and incorporated learning centers and individualized reading programs, raising achievement levels 20 percent. Students displayed significant improvements in self-esteem as reading levels and confidence increased.

Management Assistant—Lee Inc., Culver, 1979–1989. Training new employees brought forth my innate teaching abilities. Supervisor offered me promotion to stay. Left position to pursue profession in education.

The next applicant is relocating with many years of varied experience. This particular professional experience category was written to fit a specific opening—a physical education instructor, in a school district experiencing student-related drug problems. Although this candidate taught three subjects, emphasis centers on the physical education accomplishments and development of a drug abuse awareness program.

PROFESSIONAL ACHIEVEMENTS

Secondary Educator, Stevenson, Illinois, 1978–present.

Physical Education Instructor: Girls basketball team ranked second in state for two years. Assistant swimming coach, City Championship Title, 1987. Organized and directed after-school sports program. Instructed history and geography.

Drug Abuse Program Development: Played key role in developing 10th–12th grade drug abuse awareness, physical fitness, and nutrition program resulting in significantly increasing students' understanding, knowledge, and appreciation of healthy living. Parents praise and response was overwhelming. Program adopted by district and will be continued after my departure.

The following educator desires a career move from instructor to principal. Although most experience is teaching, a four-month position as substitute principal is highlighted. Notice that in the instruction category a general philosophy of education statement was included (one that appropriately fits a future position as principal). This example demonstrates a shifting of focus from instruction to management.

PROFESSIONAL ACCOMPLISHMENTS
MANAGEMENT
  Substitute Principal: Regular principal on surgery leave—
    Midtown Junior High, New Mexico, 1988. Multicultural,
    bilingual student body of 540. Weekly awards significantly
    improved discipline and attendance. Evaluated Special Ed-
    ucation pilot program, conducted seminar for discussion of
    results. Coordinated after school recreation program, signif-
    icantly boosting school moral and parent participation.
    Reading ability increased when staff incorporated high-
    interest materials for bilingual students.

INSTRUCTION
  Educator: Midtown Junior High, New Mexico, 1983–present.
    Math/English, 7th–8th grade. Developed language learning
    centers. Individualized math program (based on Math Our
    Way, American Mathematics Conference, 1987). Resulted in
    increasing national test scores 23 percent. Feel respect for the
    individual student, parental involvement, and building self-
    esteem through positive experiences and reinforcement are
    the keys to beneficial results.

The following is a Ph.D. candidate desiring a position as a university
professor:

PROFESSIONAL EXPERIENCE
Instructor: Teaching Assistant—Psychology, Boulder University,
    Gatlin, Oregon. 1988–present. Presented lectures in personality
    development, principles of adjustment, and social psychology.
    Excellent evaluations from students.
Research: Research Assistant—Boulder University, Gatlin, Oregon.
    Played key role in study and analysis of personality styles of
    American leaders for Dr. Eva Baker, 1986–1988.
Lecturer: Crestview Senior Citizen Center, volunteer, 1986. Presented
    series of lectures/discussions examining the psychological and
    related biological and social changes that occur in adulthood and
    old age. Their positive response made it an extremely rewarding
    experience.
Consultant: Special Project—Personality and Student Success (PASS),
    Fulmont Unified School District, 1987. Provided assistance in

acquiring and organizing materials, developed computerized format for evaluation. This successful project to be published in the *Journal of Learning*, Vol. 3, 1991.

Throughout the examples, notice that dates are not emphasized. What you do and how you do it are far more important than when it was done. Also notice the use of various category titles in the examples. (The education category was titled "Education," "Professional Studies," and "Academic Studies.") These category titles form the outline, presenting an image of you as a professional. Categories change with time, experience, personal preference, and career goals. An important guideline in choosing category titles is to use professional sounding terms instead of "volunteer", "part-time", or "summer work". "Educator" and "Instructor" sound more professional than "Teacher." Even beginners can use professional sounding titles. ("Educator" followed by the words "Student Teacher" or "Intern." "Instructor" followed by the words "Teaching Assistant" or "Graduate Field Work.") Following is a sample of professional experience titles:

Administrator	Instructor
Advisor	Lead Teacher
Assistant Principal	Lecturer
Assistant Professor	Management
Budgeting	Master Teacher
Coaching	New Programs
Committee Leadership	New Program Director
Committee Participation	Personnel Training
Conference Leadership	Principal
Consultant	Principal Teacher
Cooperating Teacher	Professor
Counselor	Program Development
Dean	Project Director
Department Head	Public Relations
Department Leadership	Research
Director	Superintendent
Educator	Supervisor
Evaluator	Tutor
Faculty Leadership	

Placement/Credentials File

The placement file, also referred to as an applicant's dossier, credentials, references, or credentials file, is a significant marketing tool for educators. (See "An Educator's References, The Placement/Credentials File" later in this chapter for a thorough understanding of the function it serves in your career search.)

To present your file on your resume, state the identification number if you have one. Include location, address, zip code, and telephone.

Examples

> PLACEMENT/CREDENTIALS FILE INFORMATION
> File # 65432—Career Planning and Placement Office, Southern University, Colton, Louisiana, 66666, (876) 543-2111.

> UP-TO-DATE-CREDENTIALS
> Available upon request from the office of Career Development, Planning and Placement—Lincoln College, 1234 Main Street, Westport, Rhode Island, 22222, (765) 432-1000.

Professional Affiliations and Activities

Dedication and commitment to one's profession is demonstrated by including a professional growth category on your resume. An employer feels people involved in such activities are willing to give time and effort in working with others to strengthen and enrich the field of education. Involvement also demonstrates a personal interest in staying abreast of current professional issues and confirms you are a continual learner in your field.

Joining and becoming actively involved in professional organizations has numerous benefits (besides looking good on your resume). Membership dues include newsletters and publications, keeping educators informed of current legislation, people and books, availability of grants and scholarships, and a calendar of activities. Activities include regular meetings as well as workshops, in-services, seminars, conventions, conferences, and special emphasis programs on various topics and concerns. Many newsletters include current employment openings and some provide job placement services.

One of the major advantages of getting involved in professional association activities is the instant connection and fellowship with other educators. This increases your professional visibility and network of contacts—a significant part of career search. Use your support system. Too many educators are loners, especially when starting out. They get locked into one grade level, within one small school, within one district. Affiliation with people at all levels gives you a clearer perspective of who you are and how you and your career fit into the whole picture. Also, as you work as a team member toward problem solving, you see strengths in others and begin building on your own.

Professional educators join professional associations.

If you are not already a member of an association, join one now. Usually students can get membership for a reduced fee. For a list of associations, most college and university libraries have the following directories:

> *National Trade and Professional Associations of the United States and Canada and Labor Unions*, Columbia Books, Inc., Washington, D.C.. Contains descriptions of 6,300 associations, 550 of which are education-related.

> *Encyclopedia of Associations*, Gale Research Co., Detroit. A directory containing 14,000 associations, 930 of which are education-related.

To present association memberships on your resume, state the full name of the organization (spelled correctly), along with the abbreviation if you wish. Also include presentations made, offices held, workshop and conference participation, committee involvement, or other significant responsibilities. Current memberships directly related to your professional objective are most significant. If you wish to add former memberships, show the dates of involvement.

Other professional activities to present on your resume include district or state curriculum writing, presentations or participation in seminars and in-services, articles published, district or state committee involvement, and any other type of participation for the enhancement of your profession.

There are many ways to present your professional affiliations and activities on your resume. An efficient way is to group them by similar categories.

Example 1

PROFESSIONAL AFFILIATIONS AND ACTIVITIES
Memberships
    Phi Delta Kappa—Member and past officer, 1981–present.
    WEA—Wisconsin Education Association, 1983–1986.

NCTM—National Council of Teachers of Math, 1987–present.
In-services
Graham Mathematics Project—1989.
Computers in Mathematics—1988.
Conferences
National Conference for Math Instructors, Seattle, Washington,
July 1989.
Southeastern Regional Institute Mathematics Conference, Port-
land, Oregon, August 1988.

Example 2

PROFESSIONAL CONTRIBUTIONS
Presentations and Publications
"Student Management—A New Look at Discipline," Presented at
National Education Conference, 1987. To be published, *Jour-
nal of Secondary Education*, June 1990.
"Secondary Education—Its Past, Its Future," Presented at
Washington Education Convention, 1988. Forthcoming book
(scheduled for release in 1992), Bakerson College Press,
Newland, Iowa.

Community and College Involvement

Employers seek educators who are actively involved members in their community and/or college. This demonstrates the ability to work with a variety of
people from all levels. If you willingly donate time and effort for the benefit
of your college and community, employers feel you would be an involved,
enthusiastic member of a school staff.

In stating your community and college involvement on your resume, give
the complete name of the organization or event, dates, special accomplishments, and positions or offices held. There are three areas of caution when
including these activities:

1. It is best not to include membership in a Greek fraternity or sorority
   (unless the particular employer was also involved in the same one).
   Do include honorary societies such as Phi Delta Kappa.
2. Beware of including political involvement, intense religious pursuits,
   or group memberships that turn some people off and could work
   against you. Legally, you cannot be discriminated against based on
   organization memberships. But remember—the hiring officials come

equipped with their own set of prejudices. You decide whether or not stating your strong involvement with a particular church, political affiliation, or group activity is worth the risk. (Some people feel they would not want to work for an employer who would not accept their personal group involvements. The choice is yours.)

3. Having too many activities indicates you join anything and everything. Selectively choose current, relevant ones—those which relate to and best support your professional objective.

Examples

COMMUNITY AND COLLEGE ACTIVITIES
Editor—*The Ridgemont Report*, college newspaper, 1988-1989.
Warner Community Theater, 1988, costume and scenery construction. Anxious to bring theater experiences into classroom drama productions.

The following applicant attended an in-service during student teaching, joined a professional association, and was involved in one extra-curricular college activity. This example demonstrates how activities can be grouped when there is not enough information in any single area to warrant a separate heading.

PROFESSIONAL ACTIVITIES AND OTHER INTERESTS
NEA—National Education Association, 1989-present.
In-service—University of Monroe Language Project, 1988. Successfully incorporated ideas from in-service into language lessons with fantastic results.
Riverview University College Choral Group—1986-1988. Presented programs for Veteran's and Children's Hospitals. Feel elementary students would benefit from performing for hospital patients.

Professional and civic activities can be grouped together:

PROFESSIONAL AND CIVIC ACTIVITIES
AESA—American Association of School Administrators, 1987-present.
National Conference for Administrators, Wilmont, Idaho, 1988.
Garnet United Way, board member 1986-present.
Kiwanis International, 1987-present.

Awards, Honors, and Grants

If you have received numerous awards, honors, scholarships, or grants, you may wish to create a special category to list them. Another way of incorporating them into your resume is by combining them with an associated activity. You could include academic awards, honors, and scholarships with the education category as the following applicant did. Begin a separate line for each honor.

Examples

EDUCATION
Bachelor of Arts, Baker University, 1988.
Dean's list four semesters, graduated Magna Cum Laude.
David P. Warner Scholarship Winner

Special awards can be listed with the event:

COLLEGE ACTIVITIES
Debate Club, 1985-1988, District Championship 1987.
Trident University Marching Band, 1984-1988.
Chosen for Rose Bowl Parade, 1988.

This example shows how to combine honors and membership associations:

COLLEGE DISTINCTIONS AND MEMBERSHIPS
Dean's list and honors student, 1985-1988.
Carter Memorial Award Scholarship, 1985.
Future Science Teachers of America, 1986-1988.
Land Conservation and Environment Club, 1988.

Special Skills, Language Competencies, Interests, Hobbies, Talents, and Travel

When considering the inclusion of special skills and interests, remember that everything you present in the body of your resume must support your professional objective. It will not benefit an applicant to create a special Interest and Hobbies category to include needlepoint, surfing, and home decorating. (unless the professional objective is teaching these three areas). With every statement you wish to include, ask yourself, "How does this relate to my professional objective?"

Selectively include skills, hobbies, interests, and talents that sell you for the position desired. Suggested areas for educators include language competencies, travel, computers, coaching, musical and artistic abilities, or special skills directly related to your specific objective. For example, portrait painting may relate to teaching art but does not relate to instructing science.

Make a separate category for these activities or incorporate them into your sales brochure in connection with other items. If the particular skill or competency is in demand for your desired position, or the ability or talent particularly "fits" the position, then by all means create a separate category to highlight it. For example, a bilingual ability would be very advantageous in some areas.

Examples

Creating a special category:

> BILINGUAL ABILITY
> Fluent in Vietnamese, facility in Spanish. Currently involved in tutoring bilingual elementary students.
> COMPUTER SKILLS KNOWLEDGE
> Used word processing skills for recording minutes of Student Council meetings and writing newsletters, Rogers University, 1988. Anxious to incorporate computer learning activities into the classroom.

Including special skills/talents with other categories:

> EDUCATION
> **Bachelor of Arts**, University of Newland, 1987, History. Earned traveling expenses for two European summers, increasing cultural awareness, enrichment, and understanding. Some reading and speaking ability in Spanish.
>
> COLLEGE ACTIVITIES
> Aerobics and Gymnastics, 1985-1988.
> Full CPR certification—Find improving students' physical condition improves mental capabilities and attitudes.
>
> COMMUNITY INVOLVEMENT
> Casa de la Mesa Community Hospital, volunteer, 1987. Three years of Spanish classes paid off. Working with Hispanic patients further increased vocabulary and fluency.
>
> PROFESSIONAL EXPERIENCE
> **Counselor**: Summer camp for disadvantaged children, 1987-88. Strong music interest led to supervising musical activities. Anx-

ious to incorporate music and drama programs into special education classroom.

In the following short paragraph, this student teacher chose to combine coaching experience (notice volunteer is not mentioned), a championship award, and an unusual interest and hobby of sports into the professional experience category.

> PROFESSIONAL EXPERIENCE
> **Coaching**: Little League, 1985-1988, 3rd-4th graders. District champions. Coaching interest and abilities created instant rapport with primary students. Developed spelling, language, and math learning activities around sports events. Third grade boys impressed that a female teacher had such sports knowledge.

Military Service

Include any military service relating directly to your professional objective. State military accomplishments in your Professional Experience category.

Educators, especially ones with limited paid teaching experience, should look carefully and creatively at positions held and work performed in the service. Many areas may relate directly to your professional objective (supervising, teaching, training, special skills, travel, language competencies).

Example

This applicant is applying for a position as a business instructor and counselor at a community college level:

> PROFESSIONAL EXPERIENCE
> **Instructor and Counselor**: U.S. Navy, 1983-1987. Teaching and counseling abilities became evident with successful organization and presentation of seminars in leadership, communications, and management training. Took full advantage of travel opportunities to Japan and Europe. Fluency in German. Facility in Japanese. Honorable discharge, 1988.

A Powerful Ending

Do not end your resume with the phrase, "References will be furnished upon request." It is understood that a professional educator will provide references. (They are located in your university or college placement/credentials file.) It is a dull, lifeless, and uninteresting conclusion for your high-impact sales brochure.

Just as a speech should contain a dynamic beginning and a powerful ending, so should your resume. Those are the parts that will be remembered. Your dynamic beginning is a quality custom-designed professional objective. In *Who's Hiring Who*, Richard Lathrop suggests writing a concluding thought that is a reflection of one's personality. This way your resume ends with a final picture of you as an interesting, unique individual, a person to meet.

Your concluding remark can be a reflection of the special personal qualities you bring to your career. It can further prove how you fit the position and meet the employer's needs. An effective ending may be an additional statement of accomplishment. If you decide to add a personal concluding remark, think it through carefully and make it count.

Examples

ATTITUDES AND OUTLOOK
Derive great satisfaction from watching my special education students acquire academic skills and grow in self-esteem. Personal goal—to inspire each individual to perform at the peak of his or her ability.

PERSONAL EDUCATIONAL BELIEF
Believe parent involvement is a key ingredient in the learning process. Individualized reading approach generated 70 percent parent response.

PROFESSIONAL EXPECTATIONS
There is potential and talent in every teenager. As a counselor in a continuation high school, my job is to find individual areas of interest and value and to give each student the confidence to nurture them into achievement.

EXPECTATIONS AND BELIEFS
My students are a continuing source of satisfaction for me. The handicapped child shines from caring support, encouragement, and positive reinforcement.

FUTURE OUTLOOK
Derive personal satisfaction in helping each high school student gain the necessary writing skills for success in college and careers.

Eighty percent of my senior students pass college entrance English exams.

PHILOSOPHY OF LEARNING

Believe every student can achieve success in science with the proper guidance, instruction, challenge, and motivation. Use hands-on activities to make science come alive for high school students.

PHILOSOPHY OF MANAGEMENT

When teachers, parents, administrators, and students understand we are a unified group, then results of permanent value will follow. Have strong belief in working together to turn vision into reality.

Sample Resumes

The following pages contain complete resumes based on our guidelines and suggestions. Use them for guidance and motivation in creating your own personal advertisement.

The first resume represents a beginning elementary educator. It is followed by a secondary history instructor seeking a move from Washington to Montana, and finally, an upper-grade elementary educator desiring a career move into special education. (For higher education and administration candidates, see resume samples in chapters 5 and 6.)

Erin B. Salzman

111 Monterey Lane
Collegeville, California 40000

Home: (800) 999-8777
Message: (800) 666-5444

PROFESSIONAL OBJECTIVE

ELEMENTARY EDUCATOR: Prefer grades 1-4, willing to teach other levels, where there is a need for dynamic, hands-on, motivational teaching techniques in which creativity, character-building programs, parental involvement, and team teaching experience will be utilized to fullest advantage.

CERTIFICATION

Multiple Subject Teaching Credential, California, December 1989.

PROFESSIONAL STUDIES

Bachelor of Arts, Northern University, Child Psychology Major, December 1989. Dean's Honor Roll. Donald Baker Scholarship Award.

PROFESSIONAL EXPERIENCE

Educator: Student teacher, first grade—Myers Elementary School, Sonoma, CA, 1989. Evaluated students' abilities to target needs. Incorporated motivating lessons and activities to solve specific learning problems. Used word processing knowledge for tracking progress. Master teacher valued such accurate records. Presented progress reports to parents, communicating all achievements and needs in positive manner. Involved in team teaching experience to incorporate hands-on math manipulatives and learning centers, resulting in increasing weekly math test scores 26 percent.

Educator: Student teacher, fourth grade—Olive Elementary School, Parker, CA, 1990. Team teaching of math and language skills—positive results! Developed and directed Japan unit, integrating history, art, geography, music, language, and literature, culminating in performance for parents. High interest and motivation of students, plus parents' positive response most gratifying.

Instructional Aide: Aims Pre-School, Aims, CA, 1985-1988. Directed groups in various developmental and educational activities, discovering my innate ability in communicating with young people and finding their natural curiosity delightful.

PROFESSIONAL ACTIVITIES AND OTHER INTERESTS

NEA—National Education Association
Northwood Math Project, In-Service, 1988. Used activities in learning centers.
Future Educators of America Club, 1986-1989, secretary 1989.
College orchestra, three years. Enjoy bringing music activities into lessons.

PLACEMENT FILE

Number 6580—Career Planning and Placement Office, Northern University, Collegeville, California, 40000, (800) 999-0090.

AIMS AND INTENTIONS

Enjoy creating challenging ways to motivate and inspire students to perform at the peak of their abilities. Parent involvement important. During student teaching, 75 percent of parents involved in students' reading Olympics program.

CHRIS A. COMPTON

1001 Arlington Lane   (900) 433-3344 (home)
Meadville, Washington 90000   (900) 544-4455 (message)

PROFESSIONAL OBJECTIVE

SECONDARY LEVEL HISTORY INSTRUCTOR: Preference for juniors and seniors, but willing to teach other levels where there is an opportunity to present a progressive approach in the teaching of history, geography, and government that encourages participation and involvement, and to work closely with individuals and groups to create projects to intensify understanding.

CERTIFICATION

History, grades 9-12, Montana, in progress.
History, grades 9-12, Washington, 1984.

PROFESSIONAL EXPERIENCE

Educator: American History and Government—1984-present, Maxwell High School, Maxwell, Washington, 11th-12th grades. Activity-oriented, lecture-discussion classes. Developed group projects based on individual interests, culminating in field trip to the American Historical Museum. Initiated an American history and government section in school newspaper—supervised students involved in creating first-person articles. Staff and parents praised work, community newspaper published several. History Department Curriculum Committee, 1987-89.

Extra-curricular Drama Presentations: Originated American Historical Drama Club, Maxwell High. Thirty seniors developed skits based on American historical figures. Art students participated with costumes, make-up, and scenery. Students' enthusiasm and parent and staff involvement made it an extremely successful project.

Counselor: Summerset Youth Camp—1986-present, Mountainside, Washington. Entire family participates each year. Organized activities and projects for twenty adolescents, based on forest ecology and conservation. Results: Increased students' self-esteem and enthusiasm, developed rapport and understanding between community and youth.

PROFESSIONAL PREPARATION

Graduate Studies: Twenty units towards Education Master's Degree, Riverview University, Washington, 1987-present.
Bachelor of Arts, History—Riverview University, Washington, 1984. Edited campus newspaper. All A's in history classes.

PROFESSIONAL AFFILIATIONS AND ACTIVITIES

Phi Delta Kappa, 1985-present, Special Activities Chairman, 1988.
WEA—Washington Education Association, 1984-present.
National History Educator's Conference, Aston, Washington, 1987.
Western Regional Historical Conference, Burbank, California, 1988.

UP-TO-DATE CREDENTIALS

File #54490—Educational Placement and Career Services,
Riverview University, Newbury, Washington, (900) 777-8555.

SAM E. JOHNSTON

333 Los Alamos Lane   Smithville, Texas 77777   (500) 777-9999

PROFESSIONAL OBJECTIVE

EDUCATOR FOR EDUCATIONALLY HANDICAPPED STUDENTS: Prefer grades 4-6, willing to teach other levels, where there is a need for an individualized curriculum in a positive learning environment, which is conducive to personal academic progress and building of self-esteem.

QUALIFICATIONS

M Motivate—Hands-on math activities, creative language and reading centers.
  A Assignments based on individual needs and differences.
    I Inform—Keep parents up to date with weekly progress reports.
      N New programs—Computers, music, art, and drama.
S Self-esteem—Special character building lessons to enhance feelings of worth.
  T Team member—Close communication with regular classroom teacher.
    R Reinforcement—Learning includes follow-up activity centers.
      E Evaluation—Continuous progress analysis to spot individual needs.
        A Accomplishment and Achievement—Through personal goals.
          M Monitor and Modify—To meet new objectives.

CERTIFICATION

Special Education Credential, Educationally Handicapped, Texas, 1989.
Elementary Education Credential, Texas, 1987.

PROFESSIONAL EXPERIENCE

Educator: Fourth grade, Pulmont Elementary School, Pulmont, Texas, 1987-present. Incorporate language, math, reading, art, social studies, and science activity centers into daily lessons. Students work individually and in cooperative learning groups to meet goals. Results: students' enthusiastic response, parents' involvement, and reading and math national test scores improving 37 percent. Mainstreaming educationally handicapped students into my classroom brought about strong interest in working with special students on a permanent basis.

Counselor: Summer Camp—Alpine School for Handicapped Children, 1988. Saw first-hand how understanding, caring, and active participation with handicapped children brings positive results in confidence and self-esteem.

ACADEMIC STUDIES

Eighteen units towards Master of Arts Degree in Special Education, Lawford University, Concentration on educationally handicapped students.
Bachelor of Arts, Lawford University, Child Psychology major, 1987.

PROFESSIONAL AND CIVIC ACTIVITIES

NEEC—National Educators of Exceptional Children, 1988-present.
Junior Achievers of America, district advisor, 1985. Generated interest in teaching.

PLACEMENT/CREDENTIALS FILE

Career Development Office, Lawford University, 234 Belmont Ave, Newport, Texas, 55444, (877)666-0999, File No. 57687.

ATTITUDES AND BELIEFS

Gain personal satisfaction when inspiring handicapped students to achieve in academics and gain self-confidence in their own abilities.

INTRODUCING YOURSELF TO THE EMPLOYER

Business Letters

To contact employers, professional educators use business letters directed to the individual responsible for hiring. Some are written for the purpose of gathering employment information. Others accompany a resume or application form. Letters also follow an exchange of information or materials.

Do not underestimate the significance of these letters and the impact they have on your success in the marketplace. Unlike the application form and the resume, a letter does not answer direct questions, fill in the blanks, or outline your qualities. Your letter is you communicating in sentences. The employer views business letters as a firsthand demonstration of your written communication abilities—an important professional skill for educators.

Whether a first-time applicant or an experienced educator, success in your career search depends on your ability to write clear and concise business letters. This section is designed to provide you with an understanding of the role business letters play in the screening process, along with guidelines for composing effective ones. Other business correspondence (appreciation for an interview, acceptance or rejection of a position, and notification of employment) will be addressed in later sections.

Basic Guidelines

Although we strongly recommend tailoring each resume to fit the specific position, many times applicants send an exact resume copy to several different employers. That approach, however, does not work for a successful business letter. Whatever the purpose of your letter, each one must be *individually typed and personally directed to a specific hiring official*.

Like resumes, many letters contain much of the same information. The first step in giving each one a personal touch is by using the name and correct title of the hiring official on the outside envelope, inside address, and salutation. Do not assume that only superintendents screen and hire, and never begin a letter "Dear Sir," or "To whom it may concern." School district names, addresses, and hiring officials can be found in state or national education directories available in your college placement office or library. One such resource is the *Directory of Public Schools in the U.S.*, published by the Association for School, College and University Staffing, Inc. (ASCUS).

Another way to obtain this information is to call the district. Tell personnel you are writing a letter and wish to obtain the correct name and title of the hiring official for secondary education (or appropriate department). Do not assume anything. For example, there are many ways to spell and address

Johnson. Is it Dr. Jonsen, Miss Jonsin, or Mr. Johnsen? It is also appropriate to use the title and surname on the salutation: Dear Superintendent Jonson.

This one-page sales brochure must be "letter perfect"—neatly typed, logically organized, and concise. Use complete sentences with correct grammar, punctuation, spelling, and sentence structure. This is professional correspondence, therefore use 8½" x 11" good quality white or off-white business stationery that matches your resume and envelope. Use a standard business letter format, including the full name and title of the school administrator and district address.

Cover Letters—Your First Contact

Your first contact with a hiring official is often made with a business letter accompanying your resume. The purpose of this cover letter is to introduce you and your resume to the employer and to add personal interest in you as a unique individual.

Preparation and planning is needed to develop an attractive, natural, and well-organized sales letter, to spark an employer's interest. Some applicants spend adequate time and effort on a resume, then include a hastily written, poorly prepared cover letter. These important sales brochures work together in presenting your professional image. Think of your cover letter as adding a powerful and influential personal element to your resume.

This marketing tool is the first sales brochure the hiring official sees and, consequently, carries great impact. Based on it, the employer formulates an immediate impression. An inferior letter can mean your resume is never considered.

Employers know why resumes and cover letters are sent. For an effective one, clearly communicate your potential value in an interesting and convincing way, showing what you can do for the employer. Without repeating exactly what was said in your resume, emphasize and expand on an area that makes you a particularly suitable applicant. Bring out new facts to show how you might fit in, solve a problem, or make a contribution. Then refer the employer to your resume for further facts.

Another way to create a high-impact cover letter, which stands out from the hundreds of other letters, is to prove you have done your homework. Briefly describe what you know about the position, district, or community. Mention a mutual personal contact or make a comment about a recent current event. Making a strong statement of association with the district or vacancy creates interest and positive attention by forming a connection with the employer.

Many times applicants write glowing letters presenting their current experience, yet do not sell their qualifications for the desired position. This is especially true for career changers, such as instructors desiring a move into administration. Always highlight your experiences and abilities that sell your potential for the desired position, showing you are qualified and ready for the new challenge.

Like your resume, your first cover letter is the most difficult and time-consuming. First, understand the guidelines. Next, develop your own basic model. From then on, modify—tailoring the information that relates to each unique situation.

There are two types of cover letters—letters of application and letters of inquiry.

Letters of Application

Letters of application are written in response to an announced vacancy. Begin by clearly identifying the position, your personal interest in it, and how you learned of it.

In the body of your letter, present your most marketable qualifications, special abilities, personal qualities, experience, and accomplishments that are particularly relevant to the employer's needs and that match the specific position. Obtaining a job description, or an announcement of vacancy, is extremely helpful in tailoring your letter.

In your final paragraph, ask for an interview and clearly state where you can be reached. Even though your telephone number is on your resume, it is possible these two documents can become separated. If applying out of your area, indicate willingness to travel for an interview and also to relocate, if applicable. A completed application form may be included with your letter and resume, or you may request one to be sent to you.

Letters of Inquiry

Letters of inquiry are used in gathering information. Sent early in the job search, these letters are used to locate current or expected vacancies and to inquire about application procedures.

Because you are not applying for a specific position, your letter contains a more general overview of your qualifications. Begin by stating your reason for writing. Refer to your enclosed resume and highlight accomplishments, background, and personal qualifications that fit the district or the community in general. Instead of concentrating on one particular area, show a wider breadth of knowledge and experience, in order not to limit employment possibilities.

Request an application form and inquire if other materials are needed.

Express a desire for a meeting at the employer's convenience. A letter of inquiry is not always acknowledged. To increase your chances of a response, include a self-addressed stamped envelope. Sometimes applicants are sent a form letter or an application as acknowledgement.

Upon receiving an application form and/or a vacancy list in response to a letter of inquiry, reply with a letter of application. Thank the employer for the acknowledgement. Then highlight your most marketable qualifications and personal qualities matching the specific position you desire.

Sample Business Letters

The following samples are for motivation and support. Use them as guidelines in developing personal business letters to fit each situation. These sample letters are based on the resumes in the previous section.

The first one is a letter of inquiry, written by Erin Salzman (refer to her resume for background). Erin uses her supervising teacher as a point of contact and highlights her general background and experiences, in order not to limit her employment possibilities.

Next is a letter of application based on the resume by Sam E. Johnston. Sam desires a career move into special education. This letter of application is written in response to an advertised vacancy.

Our final sample presents Chris A. Compton's second letter to the employer. (The first one, a letter of inquiry, resulted in the employer sending an application packet and a vacancy notice.) This third sample demonstrates a combination thank you, plus a letter of application for the vacancy listing.

Sample Letter of Inquiry

October 2, 1989

111 Monterey Lane
Collegeville, California 40000

Dr. Harriet Hamilton
Superintendent
Desert Cove Unified School District
333 Edgar Lane
Desert Cove, California 55555

Dear Dr. Hamilton:

Jane Harris, a former instructor in your district and currently my supervising teacher, recommended I contact you. I am writing to inquire if you anticipate any elementary teaching vacancies in the fall for which I might be considered. As an honor student, I will receive my Bachelor of Arts degree in Child Psychology and my teaching certification in December.

Jane told me you are a growing district with strong interests in open classroom and team teaching learning environments. My student teaching assignments have provided me with team teaching opportunities in both primary and upper grades. As an actively involved team member, I participated with three other teachers to target students' needs in math and English. We developed small group and individualized instruction centers to reach objectives. There was significant improvement on weekly test scores. As well as regular classroom activities, my strong computer knowledge was useful in assisting students on an individual basis in the computer lab.

As you can see from my resume, teaching has been a part of my life since 1985, when I was employed as an instructional aide. I look forward to sharing my enthusiasm, specialized training, and professional experience with the Desert Cove Unified School District.

If there are any positions for which I might be considered, please send application materials and information in the enclosed envelope. I would also like to have the opportunity to talk with you and can be reached at (800) 999-8777, or (800) 666-5444. Thank you.

Sincerely yours,

Erin B. Salzman

Enc.

Sample Letter of Application

November 15, 1989

333 Los Almos Lane
Smithville, Texas 76543

Mr. Elliot Anderson
Director of Special Education
Eastern School District
456 Pleasant Street
Lansdale, Texas 76543

Dear Mr. Anderson:

The Lawford University Career Development Office notified me of a current vacancy in your district for a special education instructor of educationally handicapped students. I am very interested in this position and would like to be considered a serious candidate for your opening.

I graduated from Lawford University, with a major in Child Psychology. My certification in Special Education is completed, along with more than half the requirements for a Master of Arts degree. As you will note on the enclosed resume, I have enjoyed the challenge of working with educationally handicapped students who were mainstreamed into my fourth grade classroom.

Reading the *Lansdale City Tribune*, I noticed your special education department has incorporated new individualized math and English programs into the curriculum. As you will see from my resume, I also use a learning environment based on student needs, incorporating activity centers for individualized and small group instruction. This has proven to be a very successful program. Our educationally handicapped students have made significant improvements in self-esteem, along with academic achievement in reaching objectives.

With your large multicultural student population, you may also be interested in knowing I work with students of varied ethnic, social, and economic backgrounds. I am enclosing a copy of my resume. Please send me a formal application form. I would welcome the opportunity to talk with you to discuss this position in detail. I can be reached at (500) 777-9999.

Sincerely,

Sam E. Johnston

Enc.

Sample Thank You and Letter of Application

March 9, 1989

1001 Arlington Lane
Meadville, Washington 90000

Mr. Kelly Grant
Personnel Director, Secondary Education
Waterford Unified School District
778 Safford Drive
Whittier, Montana 66666

Dear Mr. Grant:

Thank you so much for your quick response to my letter of inquiry, the listing of your current vacancy for the coming school year, and the formal application packet. I am very interested in the high school teaching position in the Waterford District and would like to be considered a serious candidate for the opening.

I noticed the responsibilities listed on the vacancy announcement include curriculum development. My varied professional experience is detailed on the enclosed resume, but I do wish to point out my background includes extensive curriculum development. I have served on the history curriculum committee for the past two years as our department introduced coursework incorporating drama, cultural studies, literature, and current events. This successful program was based on the information we gathered while attending seminars and workshops for history educators, presented by the Washington Education Association.

I feel my academic background and experience in history education would permit me to make a strong contribution as an instructor with the Waterford District. I am returning the completed application form, along with another copy of my resume. As requested, you will receive a copy of my college placement file.

I am traveling to Montana at the end of the month and would be pleased to arrange a meeting with you to discuss this position in detail. If further information is needed, please feel free to contact me at (900) 433- 3344 or (900) 544-4455. I look forward to your reply.

Sincerely yours,

Chris A. Compton

Encs.

REFERENCES

The Placement File / Credentials File

During your career search, letters of reference and evaluative statements must be readily available to submit to prospective employers. Unlike business and industry, the professional educator relies on the use of a college placement file as a holding station for these materials (also referred to as an applicant's Credentials File, Credentials, References, or Dossier).

When requested, the information in your file is duplicated and copies are mailed to potential employers. This professional package is a type of portfolio. It becomes another important sales brochure. The file can be used throughout your career and is a permanent record of your educational employment.

A college placement file is a convenient, time-saving tool. Without it, a candidate would be required to collect letters of reference and copies of evaluations for each potential employer. It is not unusual for applicants to apply for 50 positions. You can see how beneficial it is to have all information easily accessible and in one location. Establishing a file with a college or university is vital for success in the educator's job market. It is almost impossible to be employed in public or private schools without one. The data contained in this dossier is a significant part of the screening and employment process.

Establishing and Maintaining a File

Each college has its own rules, regulations, instructions, guidelines, and fees on establishing and maintaining a file. Generally, a student registers with the university or college career placement center to open one at the beginning of a certification or graduate program.

Many people attend different institutions to complete additional graduate work or certification requirements at various times in their career. When en rolled in a new college program, you may either have your original file transferred or establish a new, more current file with your present college. The general rule is to maintain your file with the college granting the highest level of education or the one offering the best placement services to meet your needs. Consolidate all materials at one location to avoid confusion. *Do not actively use more than one file.* University and college career placement offices only hold and issue copies of materials as requested. They do not gather information for you. It is your responsibility to keep your file up-to-date.

In this time of frequent career changes, it is wise to request a letter when an immediate supervisor leaves. Update your file every two or three years with an evaluative statement from supervisors or professors. Include other relevant information (such as responsible positions held in professional associations, documented by the organizational leader). When applicable, add new degree and certification information and changes in address, name, or job. Also, delete unrelated, out-of-date materials. Generally, this means material over six years old.

> *Never send irrelevant, out-of-date information to a prospective employer. It has little marketable value and reflects unfavorably on you.*

Confidential vs. Nonconfidential Files

In 1975, the Family Rights and Privacy Act became effective. This law states that a person has the option of establishing either a confidential or a nonconfidential file. With a confidential file, you may not read the contents. A nonconfidential file is open for your inspection. The law also states that the person creating the file determines who has the right to request its release. Some colleges offer the choice of confidential or nonconfidential references, while others provide only one option. There are arguments for both sides.

Some people claim confidential files are preferred by employers, as they display an honest report of strengths and weaknesses. Others have valid arguments for nonconfidential references. They confirm open files not only display a direct and straightforward report, but also provide self-understanding and marketing information useful to the applicant. In addition, awareness of limitations gives applicants the chance to improve and enrich their qualifications. A few states have restrictions stating confidential files are not accepted by employers.

Think carefully about which type of file you prefer and recognize the trend nationally is toward nonconfidential references. When asking for letters, inform your references if your file is confidential or nonconfidential.

What Belongs in a Placement File?

This professional package consists of academic and professional references, evaluations, personal information provided by the applicant, and other career and professionally related data.

Student teaching evaluations are usually forwarded to your file. It is your responsibility to make sure all other materials are submitted. Some placement offices ask you to include a resume. If so, resumes are normally used for counseling purposes only. They are usually not copied and forwarded to the employer with other materials. It is your job to personally present your tailored resume and cover letter to each hiring official.

At most institutions, transcripts are *not* part of your file. By law, transcripts are sent to employers to prove your completion of degree work. They are mailed when requested by the applicant. Many placement offices, however, do require inclusion of educational information found on transcripts. This is your chance to market your undergraduate or graduate education. The employer skims this information to get an overall picture of your academic background and exposure.

In submitting educational background for your placement file, use an organized outline, stating courses completed, in progress, and anticipated. This is not a legal document, but do include every course. Omit failures, withdrawals, and other courses not completed, since they did not become a part of your experience or background. This information must match your transcripts (if the employer ever decides to check). However, this is yet another sales brochure, so do not merely list courses as they appear on a transcript. Use the opportunity to categorize your academic history into marketable, readable groupings. Use an arrangement that creates the best sales package. Do not use the course number (e.g., English 301); use the course title (e.g., English, Children's Literature) instead.

Example

Courses	Semester Units	Grade
HUMAN DEVELOPMENT		
Adolescent Development	3 units	B
Self-Confidence in Adolescents	3 units	A
Learning and Communication Disabilities	4 units	In progress
HISTORY		
Mexican Civilization	3 units	B
History of Mexico	3 units	A
History of California	3 units	C
Ancient Mesoamerican Civilization	4 units	In progress
Early American History (Anticipated Fall 1990)		

By the way, everyone should own a personal set of transcripts from every educational institution attended.

A separate form is used for graduate work and postbaccalaureate teacher certification courses. Placement centers may also require statements regarding special talents and interests, unique qualifications, volunteer work, honors, travel, and employment desires. Create an organized, concise, accurate, and neat professional package. Type all information, using perfect spelling and grammar. This is another marketing tool, stamped with your professional image.

Letters of Reference

Each placement office has letter submittal regulations. Some require letters be submitted only on special forms provided by the center, then mailed directly from the writer to the college. Other career offices allow you to hand-carry letters to the center, typed on standard business stationery. However your letters are submitted, make sure they are career-related references, documenting teaching and/or management experiences. If possible, they can also include extracurricular responsibilities, unique personal characteristics, and special talents and skills.

Quality rather than quantity is the important factor in obtaining letters of reference. Beginners are usually asked to submit three letters. Two may be from your assigned supervising teacher(s) during your internships (master teacher, supervising teacher, lead teacher). It is best to request a letter of reference directly at the end of your internship, while accomplishments and qualities are easily recalled.

Additional sources are other faculty members who worked with you during student teaching, principals, department heads, college instructors, or supervisors. Former employers are a good source, if your work was in an educational setting (pre-school and public school teachers or supervisors, department heads, principals, or instructors for whom you aided or volunteered). Also consider the head of an educational organization or association, or leaders of parent/teacher organizations where you served on committees or held offices. Choose reference people carefully. Although you were a terrific employee at a fast food restaurant while in college, can your boss really support your career objective as an educator?

Experienced educators may have more letters of reference, though they should not exceed ten. Possible sources are former and current supervisors, principals or department heads, a board member, the superintendent, faculty members of colleges, members and leaders in professional organizations, or possibly a community business person.

Obviously, choose people who know you well and who are willing to support your application. It is a good idea to provide them with a brief list of your activities, responsibilities, dates of employment, or accomplishments— especially if you are not currently in direct contact with them. (In other words, remind them of your special qualities.)

Whether a beginner or an experienced educator, inform the person who is writing in your behalf as to your career intent. The reason: The most important objective of a letter of reference is to point you in the direction of your career goal. (This is especially relevant for career changers.)

An effective letter of reference highlights your unique abilities and qualities that match your desired career goal, and emphasizes your experiences and education that sell your potential for the new position.

Letters of reference are an important part of the screening process. Choose people who know you well, like you and your work, understand your objective, can speak for the quality of your work, and have strong abilities in written communication.

THE APPLICATION FORM

Some applicants give serious thought and time to creating a dynamic resume, developing an effective and interesting cover letter, collecting excellent letters of reference, and organizing marketable college placement file information. Then they submit a poorly completed application form and are out of the competition.

Each marketing tool is an important *separate ingredient* in the screening process. Your resume and the information in your college file do not take the place of an application form. Having well-prepared documents, however, will expedite and facilitate the completion of this vital marketing tool.

The application form is a weeding-out tool, not a weeding-in tool. Employers take their forms seriously and use them to narrow down applicants. Therefore, this business document is a key screening tool in selecting finalists for further consideration. You can be eliminated from the competition simply by not following directions or by not taking the time to complete it carefully, neatly, and accurately. Once you place your image on it, it becomes another one of your sales brochures.

You are in control of creating your resume—employers are in control of creating and designing their own application forms. Forms may vary but most ask much of the same information. Every question has a purpose. It is used to locate information quickly and easily.

Application forms require information on institutions attended, degrees and certification earned, possible major and minor areas of study, educational courses, professional experience, and student teaching assignments and locations. You may also be asked to indicate preferences in positions or grade levels. Indicating a variety of levels does not limit your employment opportunities.

Example for elementary level:	First choice	Primary
	Second choice	Intermediate
	Third choice	Upper

Some application forms present a list (or ask you to make a list) of extracurricular activities of interest. It is to your advantage to indicate willingness to become involved in additional projects.

You may also be asked to include a handwritten personal statement. This is a demonstration of your written communication abilities. An employer evaluates your statement for the following:

Penmanship
Grammar and spelling accuracy
Writing skill and style
Organization of information
Comprehensive presentation of material
Clarity and conciseness
Creative thinking

Take time to think your statement through and prepare it carefully. Then write forcefully what you truly believe.

Application forms can be obtained in response to business letters and resumes, or you can acquire them in district offices or during job fairs. Many are long and detailed. Completing them is a tedious job, especially when the applicant knows the same information is on the resume and placement file. A word to the wise: *Read each application form carefully and follow the directions accurately.*

Guidelines for Completing Application Forms

The following guidelines may seem simple and obvious. Take this information seriously if you wish to be a final candidate.

1. Before beginning, read the entire form to become familiar with the range and extent of information needed. Then follow the directions completely, accurately, and with care. A sloppy, incomplete application form displays lack of respect for the district.

2. Neatness and legibility are crucial. Type all answers, unless the directions say otherwise. If asked for a handwritten response, use your

best cursive writing in black ink. Do not add cute gimmicks, such as using purple ink or drawing happy faces. Remember, you are giving more than just information. The way you present yourself on paper tells the employer "this is the kind of person I am." This document is another reflection of your professional image.

3. Complete the application thoroughly. If a question is not applicable, put N/A (Not Applicable) or use three dashes (---) to show you have no information to provide. Never leave an answer blank. The employer may think you either carelessly missed it, are not intelligent enough to figure out the answer, are trying to hide something, or you do not think it is important. (The employer does think it is important or it would not be on the form.)

4. Never write "see attached resume," or "information in placement file," or "see transcripts." Employers use application forms to collect quickly and efficiently standard information in a uniform manner, and to compare relevant data on all applicants.

5. Use abbreviations and acronyms sparingly. This is another sales brochure, so clearly state information that sells you. Being a member of the AAMI does not mean anything to a board member or a screening committee member not involved directly in your particular field. Place the title of the association in parentheses after the acronym: AAMI (American Association of Mathematics Instructors).

6. If expecting your degree or certification, indicate that it is anticipated. Example: Master of Arts degree, English, to be granted May 1991, Northern State University, Rigemont, Washington.

7. Keep a copy of this completed form. You will want to review the information before an interview. It can serve as a aid for completing other application forms. Also, some application forms include instructions regarding the next step, such as requesting transcripts, college placement files, or a copy of your certification.

8. Sign and date the form. In doing so, you are stating all information is accurate and current. This is your first legal document in the application process.

SUMMARY

Resumes, cover letters, application forms, and your placement/credentials file serve as important marketing tools in the screening and application process. This chapter explained the function and significance of your paperwork and provided step-by-step guidance in preparing concise and dynamic sales brochures.

The next step is to use effectively these marketing tools to find your right career fit. Chapter 3 outlines the necessary steps for an organized job search campaign, describes available resources, explains and emphasizes the importance of thorough market research, and reviews state certification information.

CHA**3**TER

Searching for the Right Position
The Investment

S earching for the right position is an investment of time, effort, and money. It requires careful planning and hard work. You need knowledge of your job market and awareness of all available resources. An organized plan of approach, with concrete goals, must be performed with timing, consistency, and perseverance.

Your efficiency in managing this process is directly correlated to the results you can expect. Remember, 70 percent of your job search success depends on knowledge and implementation of the correct marketing skills during an active job market—doing the right things at the right times. Searching for a position is a full-time job. If you are currently working or participating in an internship or student teaching assignment, overtime is essential. At this busy time in your life, ask yourself:

"Do I really want the best possible position—the one that fits me?"
"Am I willing to work for it?"

If the answers are "Yes," there is no time for complaining and procrastination. Reaching your goal requires full energy and dedicated determination. This personal investment cannot be taken lightly, for the results have lifelong implications. We are a product of our decisions. A career move *will* change your life.

When facing a seemingly overwhelming task, educators teach students a standard reliable procedure:

- Gain knowledge of the process involved.
- Break it down into a workable sequence of small steps.

- Use all support systems and resources available.
- Learn from mistakes.
- Keep trying until success is achieved.

This is the perfect strategy when searching for a position. Like any task—some people succeed and some do not. The difference lies in knowing what you want, what to do to get it, doing your homework to make it happen, and using the process as a learning experience. People who fail do not lack the desire to make things happen. They lack the knowledge, skills, an organized plan of action, and personal commitment.

This chapter provides the basic information for developing and implementing a successful job search campaign. However, this chapter is information only. To make it happen, *you* must add the essential human ingredient. Success happens only to those who are willing to make a personal investment in conscientious planning, determined effort, and steadfast commitment toward their goal.

JOB SEARCH STRATEGIES

Steps for a Successful Move into the Marketplace

Start Early—Follow Directions

Searching for a position is a time consuming activity. Timing itself is a crucial factor in the educator's job market. Therefore, an early start is essential. For beginning educators, early is at the end of your first phase of student teaching or internship, or at the beginning of your second stage. Begin resume writing, assemble placement file materials, become familiar with your career placement center, gather information on openings, collect references, identify desired school districts, outline plans, and begin your move into the marketplace. If you wait until after graduation to start, most districts are well on their way in the hiring process, and you miss 80-90 percent of the activity.

A way of getting started is to inquire early about possible openings and gather knowledge on each district's application procedure. Write, call, or visit district administration offices to get this information. Find answers to these questions:

- Are teaching (or administration) applications currently being accepted?
- What is the application procedure?
- When will the employer begin conducting interviews?
- What is the procedure for scheduling interview appointments?

Remember, each district has its own screening and application requirements. One may request only a completed application form. Another may want a resume, cover letter, transcripts, and a copy of your college placement (or credentials) file.

> *Comply promptly and accurately with the*
> *requirements of each individual school district.*

You can apply and interview before completing degree and/or certification requirements, as long as all conditions are met by the date of employment. The expectation date for your document(s) is stated in your paperwork. It is also not necessary for beginners to have a completed placement file to begin application. Student teachers can send partial files to prospective employers.

At the end of degree and certification programs, everyone is busy. Put your job search high on your priority list. A bright, shiny, new degree and credentials look terrific on a wall but have very little value unless put to use in your profession. Searching for a position is stressful and tedious. Entering late leads to added frustration and disappointment.

Get It Together—Organizing You

The job search process has multiple elements. The fundamentals include setting aside periods for planning, developing sales brochures, writing correspondence, making telephone calls, researching and information gathering, record keeping, accumulating references, and communicating with contacts. An efficient method of organization is an investment worth your time and effort.

Begin by setting up a work area in your home where all job search materials are located. On a table or desk keep ample amounts of stationery supplies, scratch paper, envelopes, manila folders, file labels, stamps, index cards, a dictionary, and a large calendar. Have a typewriter, word processor, or clerical assistance readily available for correspondence.

A telephone needs to be located near your work area so you can easily locate job search information when receiving or placing calls. During the height of your job search, have telephone calls received when you are not present, by an answering machine or a friend. Always keep actively moving in a forward direction. Never sit at home waiting for a call. Although employers may offer encouraging words, nothing is for sure until you sign the contract.

Get It Together—Organizing Materials

Organization of screening materials is another important aspect of preparation. A resume and cover letter, completed application form, transcripts, copies of certification, a health certificate, placement file information, and additional references may all need to be submitted during a certain time frame to many districts.

College personnel are often understaffed and have large numbers of transcript requests. Timing is vital. You miss out on the hiring process if your documents do not arrive during the application period. One way of handling transcripts, certification, and health certificates is to make clear photocopies. Have a Notary Public imprint the Notary's seal and sign for their accuracy. Never send original certification until offered a position. Inform the employer you will present original documents if hired. Have prepared sets of all documents ready when entering the marketplace.

Another method of handling transcripts is through a service called ACADEM. It is a holding house for official transcripts. There is a one time set-up fee of $35.00 and a $5.00 charge each time your file is sent. All your transcripts are stored in one place and issued in one package within forty-eight hours of your written request. This a time saver for students who have attended two or more colleges. It is accepted in all states. For further information contact:

> ACADEM
> P. O. Box 1098
> Cardiff-by-the-Sea
> California 92007-0827
> Telephone (619) 436-1695

Employers have their own methods of sorting and handling materials submitted by applicants. Therefore, do not staple documents together or place them in plastic folders or three ring binders. Submit each one as is or place them all in a manila folder or large envelope.

You may consider purchasing personalized business cards. They are relatively inexpensive, convenient to carry with you everywhere, and are extremely useful during your job search. The format can be very simple: your name, home address, and telephone number. Do not use a business, school, or district address or telephone. Logos and short statements of personal philosophy can be added. The following is an example of a business card for a new educator.

Erin B. Salzman
111 Monterey Lane
Collegeville, CA 40000
Home: (800) 999-8777
Message:(800) 666-5444

- Happiness is helping students reach
their full potential.

Create a Personal Plan of Action and Activity Schedule

Once you have an organized work area and decided on a method of handling screening materials, the next step involves creating a personal plan of action. This puts your job search in fast-forward.

A plan of action is a contract, a promise you make with yourself, to complete all necessary tasks within a specified period of time. The purpose of this procedure is to focus your efforts. It turns out to have another important benefit. A job search is emotionally draining. Working systematically, with organized written plans and schedules, helps maintain emotional stability and self-confidence during this critical period.

Begin your plan of action by identifying all prospective employers and districts of interest that fit your criteria (taken from your personal assessment—location, socio-economic level, programs offered, working and living conditions). Find district names and addresses through directories in your college career/planning center. Chances of success improve when geographical boundaries are enlarged. Apply for positions, regardless of location. You can always turn down an offer. Every interview is a learning experience. By the way, early in your job search, it is important to have interviews with districts that are not your first choice for employment. A common mistake is having your first interview scheduled with the district you want the most. The more practice you have in actual interviews, the better you will be at handling them.

List the districts of interest and tasks to complete in the application process. Describe precisely how and when you intend to complete these tasks. This draft is usually modified as one moves through the job search process. The important part in the beginning is outlining an initial plan. In writing your plan, you have taken that first step.

A desired position becomes a goal only when you begin action toward achieving it.

Example of a plan of action:

POTENTIAL EMPLOYERS (in order of preference)
1. Glendale District
2. Westview District
3. Mountainview District
4. Clearlake District
5. Crestview District
6. Woodland District
7. Lansdown District
8. Lakeside District
9. Northbay District
10. Bayshore District
11. Madison District
12. Southgate District

TASKS TO COMPLETE WITH EACH ONE
Contact districts (tell how—in person, by mail, or telephone).
Inquire about application procedures.
Obtain correct name and title of hiring official.
Read district literature. Gather information.
Step by step, follow individual requirements for application.

POSSIBLE REQUIREMENTS
Obtain and complete application form.
Return completed application form (mail or hand carry).
Submit resume and cover letter.
Order placement/credentials file information.
Order copy of transcripts.
Additional references.
Interviews.

OCTOBER PLAN OF ACTION

Every Monday and Tuesday—Lunch break—Call three districts each day to inquire about application procedures and get name of hiring officials. Evenings—Work one hour on tailoring resumes and cover letters.

Every Tuesday—After school—Visit, write, or call three district offices to get application forms and district literature. Evening—Work one hour on tailoring resumes and cover letters.

Every Wednesday—After school—Complete (type) three application forms. Evening—Work one hour on tailoring resumes and cover letters.

Every Thursday—After school—Mail (or hand carry) three application forms and/or resume and cover letter as requested. Order copies of placement file if requested.

Every Friday—Visit college career center—Get needed addresses, names and telephone numbers, gather information on school districts, inquire about job fairs, current openings, and on-campus interviews, talk to counselors, get advice on resumes.

Every Sunday—Set goals for new week.

If you are currently working or student teaching, use times before school, at lunch, after school, and evenings to work on these tasks. In your plan of action, be specific. Use real numbers, days, and times to describe how you plan to carry out each task. (e.g., Monday, write three letters after school.) Everyday do something constructive toward your goal.

At the height of the marketplace activity, use your plan of action to create an activity schedule. This technique keeps you on target and moving forward. There are many ways to design an activity schedule. Use any format that works for you. The key is to set aside time each week to review your plan, modify it, and evaluate progress. Table 3 is an example.

Keep in Touch

If you request that your placement file be sent to a district or mail an application, you can only assume everything reached the employer. If your materials did not arrive, you are not being actively considered. Therefore, it is wise to include a follow-up date on your activity schedule to make sure your materials arrived. Short of being a pest, maintain regular contact with your districts of interest. Keep your name alive in a friendly, positive sense. Have a reasonable amount of contact and follow up calls to inquire about current information, new vacancies, arrival of documents, and the status of your application. Although the district has an application with your name on it, they do not know the extent of your interest unless you show it.

If possible, make a special effort to meet the people in the personnel office. Always be polite, and businesslike, and keep them informed of your

Table 3.
Activity Schedule

	Contact Employer (Name)	Get Application Form	Return Application Form (With Resume and Cover Letter If Requested)	Name, Address, Phone, and Title of Contact Person	Order Placement File	Follow up (Making Sure All Arrived)
Weeks Oct. 1	Glendale District	10/1	10/3	Dr. Reynolds, Personnel Director 100 Avondale Lane, Rothsville, CA 22222 (700) 777-8888	10/5	10/10
	Westview District	10/2	10/4			
	Mountainview District	10/3	10/5			
8	Crestview District	10/8				
	Clearlake District	10/9				

professional goals. They can be of great assistance to you with job search information and advice. Although secretaries and office personnel do not hire educators, they may be involved in the screening of applicants. When it comes time to place your documents on the top or the bottom of a stack, or give screening input, it certainly does not hurt if they know you and like you.

Keep Accurate Records

It is not unusual to apply at twenty-five different districts. Do not trust your memory to keep track of all activities. Every potential employer may require placement file information, copies of transcripts, a resume and cover letter, a completed application form, and a screening interview. With additional interviews, visits, telephone calls, letters, and references, you can easily see why searching for a position is a confusing job.

It is imperative to stay organized. Use any method that works for you, but keep detailed records. Some applicants use a 5" x 7" index card for each position, listing all completed activities. Another technique is using an activity accomplishments list. Table 4 is an example.

Table 4.
Activity Accomplishments List

	Application Form Sent	Resume and Letter Sent	Placement File Sent	Followed up	Interviews (Date and Name of Interviewer)	Sent Thank-you	Name, Phone, Address
DISTRICT/ EMPLOYER							
Glendale District	10/3	10/3	10/5	10/10	11/5 Dr. Reynolds	11/6	Dr. Terry Reynolds Glendale School District 100 Avondale Lane Rothsville, CA 22222 (700) 777-8888
Westview District							
Mountainview District							

One additional organizational technique is keeping a separate large envelope or file folder of all correspondence to each employer. Include copies of business letters and resumes, completed application forms, and any correspondence received from each district. (Always keep a personal copy of all materials submitted.) Also note all communication, whether by mail or telephone, and indicate the results of the call or correspondence. Include personal notes following an interview (explained in chapter 4) and any other information such as names, titles, and telephone numbers of contacts or people who gave you special support.

A plan of action gets you started by identifying the necessary steps and focusing your efforts on initial goals. An activity schedule checks your progress and keeps you motivated, moving, and on track. You stay organized with an activity accomplishments list. During the stressful period of job search, peace of mind and self-confidence is enhanced when *you* take responsibility and steadily proceed in a straight-forward direction toward your goal. These job search "tools" aid your progress.

Budget Your Money

Job search requires a financial investment. Expenses for marketplace activities include the following:

Travel: These expenses occur while gathering information, applying, and interviewing. Whether personal or public transportation, it must be reliable. Local travel expenses include gas, vehicle maintenance, parking expenses, or transportation fares. Long distance travel includes air or rail fare, lodging, meals, taxis or a rental car, and gratuities. (Keep in mind most positions require more than one interview.)

Policies regarding long distance travel reimbursement vary depending on district needs, budgets, and the degree of interest in a particular applicant. Sometimes part or all travel expenses are paid by the employer. Other times it is the applicant's total responsibility. Who pays expenses is discussed at the time of the interview request. If the employer reimburses, keep detailed records so you have an honest accounting. In any event, budget travel money for your job search. If applying for fifty openings, it can add up to a sizable amount—especially for long distance interviews.

Telephone: Expenses include local, toll, and/or long distance calls. An answering service may be required during the height of job search.

Professional Appearance: At all times during your job search, look like a professional. Businesslike clothing, shined shoes, and a conservative haircut (for both men and women) is essential. A Murphy's Law for applicants could be the following:

> *The one day you hand-carry a completed application form to the district in ragged jeans and shabby T-shirt is the day you are introduced to the hiring official.*

Correspondence Materials: Expenses include resume and cover letter typing and printing, typewriter or computer costs, envelopes, stationery materials, and postage (regular, special handling, or registered).

Fees: Many career centers have registration fees. There are duplicating charges for transcripts, documents, and certification; testing fees; and member-ship dues in professional organizations.

Nothing is free anymore—including getting a job.

Who Is Going to Find You a Job?

The telephone book has numerous listings of private employment agencies in the business of finding jobs—for a fee. Some work exclusively with educators. Agencies with branches around the country can be helpful if you are looking for a job in another area.

If you decide to use a private agency, read your contract carefully before signing. Know the types of positions they handle, get a clear understanding of the fees involved, and check their reputation with former customers. Remember, private employment agencies are in the business to make money. Career satisfaction is your first priority, not theirs. Using the private employment agency approach, you have a one percent chance of finding your right career fit.

Every state has a public employment service with local offices in larger communities. They are listed in your telephone book under state government listings. Since they are operated by state governments, they are tax-supported and have no fees. Nationwide, this gives you a 3 percent chance of success.

Responding to want ads in Sunday editions of newspapers increases your chances to 5 percent. (The Midwest and the Great Lakes areas do advertise. However, most school districts do not.)

Although college placement centers offers valuable services and information, they also have a large and varied student population to serve. Putting your career search solely in their hands increases your chances to only 6 percent.

An improvement over these methods is a common sense technique called direct contact. You focus your personal effort on directly contacting employers, inquiring about openings, and introducing and making yourself known. This process involves your shoe leather, your telephone, your car and gas, your typewriter and stamps, your energy and perseverance. However, your chance of success jumps to 24 percent.

And better yet is a method called networking. This basically means people working with people. You use all possible contacts to let people know who you are and what you want. Gradually, like links on a chain, each new connection enlarges and expands your network. Networking increases your probability of success to 48 percent.

Locating Sources—Surveying the Marketplace

In surveying the marketplace, there are many sources and resources available to you. Success depends on identifying and using all of them. These sources can be divided into a paper network and a people network.

The Paper Network

The paper network is a result of the equal opportunity and affirmative action laws affecting our tax supported institutions. Basically, the law says employment openings in education are to be announced for a minimum of three days. All public schools recognize the significance of this law and publicize openings.

Unfortunately, the law does not state where the positions are to be advertised. Consequently, not all school districts publicize their positions widely. If a last minute unexpected opening occurs, the position may indeed be announced for three days—but very briefly, and possibly only on district bulletin boards or marqués, in order to shorten the screening and hiring process.

Be aware that while some employers advertise extensively, others almost never publish widely. As a result of the equal opportunity and affirmative action laws, however, we now at least do have published openings. This has greatly influenced and expanded our paper network for professions in education. Listed below are some sources of the paper network:

Media. Some employers advertise in local Sunday newspapers. *The New York Times, Wall Street Journal*, and newspapers in other major cities often contain vacancies. Television, and radio are also sources for job opportunity information. Watch for areas with increasing school enrollments, retirements, promotions, and new school openings.

Professional Associations. Association publications such as newsletters and journals contain job vacancies. Some also provide placement services. (See the section in chapter 2 on professional affiliations.)

Publications. Publications such as *The Chronicle of Higher Education, Change: The Magazine of Learning*, and *Education Week* include career information and job opportunities. The *Affirmative Action Register* and *Academic Journal* are two publications that contain only job listings.

Federal Government. Government agencies such as the Job Corps, the Department of Education, and the Department of Defense are a source of employment. Your local Federal Job Information Center can help you locate vacancies for educators and assist you with application procedures.

State Employment Agencies. Some state education agencies mail lists of openings in their state. These addresses can be found in your college career center or by calling the state education office.

Private Schools. *The Handbook of Private Schools* and *Boarding Schools* are two sources containing addresses of nonpublic institutions. Although salaries are lower, this may be offset by the advantage of smaller class size and other benefits.

Bulletin Boards. Watch for vacancy listings posted on bulletin boards of university departments, district offices, individual schools, and career centers.

College Career/Placement Centers and Career Libraries. Published openings are an important part of college placement and career centers. Each center has its own system of informing applicants of these vacancies. Many have vacancy lists and notebooks containing openings categorized by areas, grade levels, subjects, administration, special education, overseas employment, and higher education. Some centers publish and send vacancy bulletins to applicants on mailing lists. Placement offices often have a Dial-A-Job or Job Hot Line service with recordings of recent vacancies.

Career centers and libraries contain a wealth of descriptive occupational materials and up-to-date information, including data regarding public and nonpublic schools and public service organizations such as private learning centers, government agencies, business and industry, non-profit organizations, and overseas opportunities.

Career centers have application forms, salary schedules, job descriptions, taped interviews, information on hiring opportunities according to geographic areas, and employment trends. One can often obtain names of alumni willing to be contacted and provide insight and information. Employers contribute recruitment literature and general information to career centers—sometimes on videos, slides, or tape programs.

Centers provide a multitude of programs and services. They offer individual counseling services, graduate school advisement, information on career alternatives for educators, and career related seminars and workshops. During the height of your job search, visit your college career/placement center weekly to stay abreast of new information and openings.

Direct Contact through the Mail. This is an important part of the paper network. You are introducing yourself and inquiring about possible openings with letters, resumes, and application forms. Use directories in your career centers to locate school districts and names of employing officials (whether in your home state or other states). Contact them, present yourself, and make your needs, wants, and availability known.

A widely used reference source is the *Directory of Public School Systems in the U.S.*, published by ASCUS. Addresses can also be found in city libraries, the state department of education, and the local yellow pages.

Job Fairs. Many employers participate in job fairs as part of their recruitment efforts. These fairs are sponsored by school districts, associations, and colleges. They are usually held in convention centers, hotels, and on college campuses. Since they are planned and organized for applicants, they are part of the paper network.

Employers see recruitment fairs as a low-cost opportunity to advertise openings and meet a large pool of interested applicants. Applicants see job fairs as a unique chance to gather information and talk directly and somewhat informally with numerous district representatives on one day, in one location.

As you may guess, hundreds of applicants attend these recruiting fairs. Unprepared candidates sometimes see it as a crowded, confusing waste of time. For a profitable day, know in advance which districts are truly of interest to you. Dress professionally, be prepared with questions, gather information on application procedures, and take copies of your resume. Carry a briefcase or notebook, pen and pencil, and business cards.

Since job fair details change often, see your college career center for current information regarding dates, locations, and contact people.

On-Campus Interviewing. Campus interviews are yet another part of the paper network since they are arranged for applicants. Interested school districts notify college career centers of their needs and ask to send representatives to the campus to actively recruit educators.

Sign-ups are on a first come, first serve basis. Usually the process involves an initial paper screening, then a meeting is arranged through the placement center. (The career/placement office restricts applicants to only those who fit the employer's needs—grade levels, subject areas). On-campus interviewing is a unique chance to move immediately to the interviewing stage with minimum screening and hassle.

Employers spend time and money sending interviewers to college campuses. Those who extend the effort have enough openings to justify the investment. These districts are actively searching for candidates. Employers send representatives all over the country and overseas to recruit.

Watch for dates of on-campus interviewing. Take advantage of this opportunity to have direct personal contact with someone who has the power to hire. Even if the district is not your first choice for employment, it is a perfect time to gather information and practice interviewing skills. One never knows—a district you may not have considered could turn out to be an interesting, progressive, and growing career opportunity.

A Word of Warning: Do not think that because the interview takes place on your college campus, it is not a professional activity. The same rules apply as for a meeting at a district office. Be on time, be prepared, and be your best professional self—in appearance and demeanor. Not showing for an appointed campus interview reflects badly on the career/placement center and on the university—but mostly on you as a professional.

The People Network

Referrals. Referrals are part of the people network—people knowing people. We believe 40 percent of each graduating class ends up where they are because of referrals through personal contacts. Employers prefer to hire educators they know or know about.

Make your availability and career goals known to principals, supervising teachers, faculty, your career/placement center staff, neighbors, friends, former employers and business associates, relatives, secretaries, and local business people. Keep your eyes and ears open. Talk to people at church, at the health club, at PTA meetings, at the doctor's office. Tell your lawyer, your banker, insurance agent, and hair dresser. Become aware of retirements, pregnancies, leaves, promotions, sabbaticals. Attend association meetings and activities. Let others know who you are and what you want. Stating the name of a personal contact in a cover letter or on the telephone creates immediate interest. (Hopefully, your contact is a well-respected individual.)

Principals. Principals often have a strong voice in the hiring process. If they know you and want you on their staff, their input can greatly influence decisions. When visiting schools, make a special effort to meet the principal(s) or department head(s). Leave your resume behind, or mail or hand-carry it the following day (tailored to meet their needs) to remind them who you are.

Part-Time Employees. Student teachers, substitutes, and short-term contract employees are many times hired on a permanent basis because they are known by students, parents, and other educators. During student teaching or substituting, get to know the other educators. Make a point of meeting and talking with the principal or department head. Part-time people who are successful in getting full-time positions are the ones who get known.

Make networking a part of your day, everyday.

     Professors and Supervisors. Keep in touch with your college professors, supervisors, and former employers from an educational setting. They often receive information regarding vacancies. Let them know your progress during your job search.

     College Career Placement Centers. College placement centers provide a people network through counseling services and referrals. Openings come in daily during the peak hiring period, and referrals can be made only if counselors know your status. Keep them informed of your progress and professional goals.

     Do not be shy about contacting people and asking for advice. Everyone at some time in their life needs the support and help of others. Use agencies, centers, services, counselors, advisors, educators, friends, and contacts. Ask questions, seek advice, request guidance—and listen. But the bottom line is that you must do it.

Success depends on your efforts—and the best results come from using your own best resource, you. You are the only one who can truly find your right career fit.

     The following resources may be helpful at some point in your job search.

Academic Journal: The Educator's Employment Magazine. The Academic Journal, Box 392, Newton, CT 06470. Published biweekly.

Affirmative Action Register. William H. Green, 105 Brentwood Blvd., St. Louis, MO 63105. Published monthly.

Boarding Schools. National Association of Independent Schools and Colleges and Secondary School Admissions Test Board, 4 Liberty Square, Boston, MA 02109. Published annually.

Chronicle of Higher Education. 1255 23rd Street, NW, Washington, D.C. 20037. An independent newspaper published weekly except the first three weeks in August and the last three weeks in December.

Directory of Public School Systems in the United States. Published by ASCUS (Association for School, College and University Staffing), 301 South Swift Road, Addison, IL 60101. Published annually.

Education Week. 4301 Connecticut Ave., NW, Suite 250, Washington, D.C. 20608. Published 42 times per year.

Handbook of Private Schools. Boston: Porter Sargent Publishing, Inc. Published annually.

Market Research

An important part of the job search process is market research. This practice consists of gathering information and evaluating the advantages and disadvantages of each school district, employer, and community of interest. Gathering knowledge allows you to tailor your sales brochures, prepare interview questions, and practice responses to best show how you meet the employer's needs. This makes you a stronger, more marketable candidate.

Market research is also essential in order to make an intelligent decision if offered a contract. The more you know about the position, the better you can answer the following questions:

Will this career move provide professional satisfaction?
Is this where I will be happy, motivated, and challenged?
Does the community match my values and interests?
Is this my best possible professional match?
Does the whole package match my personal self-assessment needs?

> ***How do I find the right answers? You find the right answers by asking the right questions.***
> —*ancient proverb*

District Information

District information can be obtained from several sources. Begin with the district personnel office. Many publish public relations materials. This information tells about the schools and their programs, their basic philosophy, socio-economic level, salary steps, fringe benefits, employee qualities sought by the district, and statistical information such as the number of students and the size of the district. Some give information regarding the hiring process. Many times school district information can also be found in the local Chamber of Commerce and university and college career/placement offices.

Newspapers and Media

Community newspapers and the media are excellent sources of information. Subscribe to the local newspapers in your geographical areas of interest. Find which districts are passing bond issues, where new schools are being built, where enrollments are increasing. This provides insight on hiring opportunities, longevity of employment, and also possibilities of salary and benefit increases.

Gather information on achievement and citizenship awards, scholastic reports, special accomplishments, and new programs. Find out about the school board—what positions do they hold in the community?

It is equally important to notice areas of conflict and strife—striking teachers, firing of principals, dissatisfied parents, problem students. Districts with dissension and friction mean different things to different people. For some, they are areas to avoid. For others, they are areas of need.

Educators, Secretaries, and Custodians

Talk to educators, secretaries, and custodians in the districts that interest you. Make an appointment to visit schools while classes are in session. Along with gathering information on the curriculum, students, and services, it is also an opportunity to find out about hiring procedures. Ask about the number and types of interviews new candidates can expect and who does the interviewing and final selection. Meet the department head and/or the principal.

Recently hired educators are an excellent source of information. They were in your position not long ago. Not only can they identify with your situation and give support, but they have gathered valuable tips during their job search, which they may share with you.

Community and District Events

Attend open houses, back-to-school nights, parent-teacher association gatherings, and school board meetings. Ideally, attend sports events, musical and drama productions, church services, yard sales, and community affairs. Find out what happens in town on Friday nights. Remember, especially in small towns, the school can be the focal point of community activities.

If moving or considering areas away from your immediate environment, talk to a local real estate agent. Prices of housing and property values are determined in large by the school district's reputation. It is a realtor's job to know popular opinion. They also know school district boundaries.

In an interview, you may be asked, "If we were to make you our high school principal, what would you do to improve our programs and solve our problems?" Would you be able to answer in an organized, convincing, and believable manner? Your homework is to do sufficient research to know the needs of the school, the district, and the community.

> *The more you know, the better prepared you are in making an intelligent career decision and successfully gaining employment.*

Letter of Introduction for Information Gathering

Student teachers have time between semesters or quarters and after final assignments for information gathering. Use this time wisely to visit districts and schools. Page 92 provides an example of a letter written by a student teacher for the purpose of gathering information.

This is a very effective way of gathering information and making important contacts. Here is a possible chance of visiting a classroom in your desired district and talking to a first year instructor who has current information regarding the hiring procedures.

Make a serious effort to meet the principal. State the reason for your visit (gathering information for possible future employment considerations). Be courteous, interested, and professional. Have questions prepared in advance and do not overstay your visit.

Sometimes applicants hesitate to visit schools, thinking they will bother someone. Remember, employers want applicants to do their homework. Visiting schools is a practical way to gather information to help find out what you want. If your meeting sparks further interest in the district, ask for a referral to another school or grade level. This is how one begins building a network of contacts. Always follow through with thank-you letters.

Information to Know

Some data is straightforward and easily obtained in reports, pamphlets, and newspapers. Other knowledge is more difficult to acquire. The following is a list of possible variables to use in considering school districts:

Sample Letter of Introduction

September 1, 1989

111 Monterey Lane
Collegeville, California 40000

Ms. Debra Harding
Educator, First Grade
Wellington School District
500 West Pennsylvania Avenue
Haverford, California 30000

Dear Ms. Harding:

My name is Erin Salzman. You were recommended by Dr. Devlin, principal of Rheinhardt School. I will graduate from Northern University and will receive my elementary teaching credential in December. My second semester of student teaching begins soon. Currently, I am gathering information on schools in the Wellington County area.

Could I visit your class during reading instruction sometime this month and talk with you for fifteen minutes during lunch or after school? As a first year teacher, I realize how busy you are. I am very willing to help with any small group or individual instruction.

I have heard wonderful things about your new literature-based reading program and cooperative learning groups and would appreciate any time you could give me. I will call this week to see if it is possible.

Thank you.

Erin Salzman
Home phone: (800) 999-8777

District. Does the geographical location match your needs? Is it an elementary, high school, or unified district? What grades are included at each level? What is the size of the district (number of elementary, junior high or middle schools, and high schools)? Is it a semester-based or year-round schedule district? Read the history, development, philosophy, and characteristics (from district literature). What is the tax and financial status of the district? Learn the size of the schools, and the socio-economic level of the students and community. Know the typical class size. Secondary educators should learn the number of classes per day. Does the district offer faculty in-service training days?

Growing Area. Is this area increasing or decreasing in population? What is their growth potential? If decreasing, what is the predicted future of this position? Although there is no such thing as total job security, some districts are more stable than others.

Read all contract conditions carefully. Be aware that some districts with declining enrollments hire educators on a temporary basis only. New educators, thrilled to be offered a contract, may not think through any long-term implications. Being hired on a temporary basis means a year-to-year contract. Continued employment depends on enrollment. The position does not lead towards tenure, and the situation may continue indefinitely. (Many times temporary educators are told each spring they may not be rehired in the fall. Each summer they wait it out.) Maybe you feel this would not affect you or bother you; the important thing is getting a job now. However, if you are interested in the prospects of long-term employment and benefits and some feeling of security, aim your efforts toward employment in growing areas. These are areas with increasing populations, where new families are moving and new homes and schools are being built.

Faculty. Know the size of faculty and departments. How many new educators are hired each year? What support is given for training and guidance of new people? How long do educators stay in the district? Find areas of faculty expertise (which also tells you areas of need). Talk to educators in the district at the grade level or subject area you desire. What are their teaching methods? How is the faculty morale? Do you feel your teaching or administration style is compatible with theirs? Why is the position open? What is the evaluation process for new educators? Do you get a team feeling from the faculty? Is there team teaching and planning? Open classrooms? What is the structure of the school or department? Is there a feeling of professionalism within the faculty? What is the current management style? What is the largest single problem facing the staff or district now?

Curriculum and Facilities. Gather all curriculum information available on your grade level(s) or subject area(s). What curriculum guidelines and materials are prescribed? What textbooks and supplementary materials are being used? What reading, math, social studies, and science programs are used? If there is a curriculum center, visit it and the school library. Inquire about AV materials, computers, and equipment for classroom use. Are materials and equipment up-to-date? Find out about new curriculum developments, pilot programs, or new programs in planning stages. Notice the newness and upkeep of facilities. If applicable, are the classrooms air-conditioned or cross-ventilated? In December, this is not important. One's priorities change in the summer with thirty students in one room, in 100 degree weather.

Students. Gather information on student placement. Are students grouped? If so, how? What is the academic, cultural, and ethnic background of students? What is the socio-economic level? What percentage are bilingual? What percentage of the high school students are enrolled in vocational versus college preparatory curricula? What kinds of discipline problems are prevalent? How are discipline and academic problems handled? Is there a standard written procedure for handling student problems?

Services. What support services and personnel are available for non-English speaking students? Nonreaders? Behavioral problems? Counseling and guidance? Speech? Is there a social worker and nurse? Librarian? Consultant? What extracurricular activities are available for students? Clubs, organizations, sports?

Community. Elementary and secondary educators need to know the level of home and community support for education. Are parents involved in their children's education? To what extent? Is there an active parent-teacher organization? Know the cost of living and housing in the community and living conditions. Locate the recreational, religious, and cultural facilities. Know the role the school plays in the community. Would you like to live in this community? Will your family be happy here? Is this an area where you would like to raise a family? Would you want *your* child attending school in this district? What are your relocation expenses? If you do not plan to live in the community, what is the travel time? (Make the trip during busy hours.) What are the transportation costs and availability? What is the climate? Where is the nearest college for continuing your education?

Salary. Get the district salary schedule. Know the entry and top level salaries. Know the benefit package and leave policies. Is there pay for extracurricular activities? Some districts reimburse educators for graduate courses or continuing education coursework. What is the district's history on salary increases? Compare it to other districts. Salary and benefits are important issues. However, your happiness with the complete picture is the key to career satisfaction.

It is not always possible to find answers to all these questions. Serious candidates gather as much information as possible. The process of gathering information should be intriguing. After all, this is your career, and the decision you make influences your entire life. Candidates who take the time and effort to gather information are the ones who market themselves effectively and make an intelligent career decision.

STATE CERTIFICATION INFORMATION AND OFFICES

State certification (or licensing) is a requirement for employment in public education. Although all hiring is done at the local level, certification is a state function. The State Board of Education (or the Department of Public Instruction in some states) reviews qualifications of applicants and issues licenses.

Beginners should apply for certification immediately after graduation or at the end of their student teaching or graduate level education program. Although colleges may offer guidance in application, it is your sole responsibility to apply for and obtain your license.

It is best to type or print carefully the information required on the application form. Follow all directions neatly and accurately. Illegible writing can result in delays in obtaining certification. Complete a separate application for each license desired. Fees are required, along with complete transcripts, academic records, and teaching experience information.

For educators planning to relocate, contact the certification office in your state of interest and begin the application process early. Upon receiving your license(s), be aware of the expiration date and renewal requirements.

State competency testing is a condition for certification. Although many states require the widely recognized National Teachers Exam (NTE), some do not. (If interested, see your career center to obtain an *NTE Bulletin of Information*.)

There is currently a move toward developing nationwide teaching standards and establishing national certification. Presently, however, each state is free to develop its own competency testing policies, regulations, and standards for passing. In addition, each state manages and controls its own certification process, creates its own application forms, and issues its own licenses.

Policies and practices change often and vary greatly from state to state. Therefore, applicants need to contact the certification office in their state of interest for testing criteria and certification information. A listing of the certification offices is located at the end of this section. In some areas, there are alternate routes to certification. There is also reciprocity (shared certification agreements) between some states.

Along with proof of certification, there are various supporting documents required at the district level before employment is official. Many require a health record, a police record check, a residency statement, and proof of United States citizenship. Applicants normally take a loyalty oath and complete various other application questionnaires and forms. See your individual district at the time of employment regarding these supplementary documents. Table 5 provides a listing of state certification offices.

Table 5.
State Teacher Certification Offices

Alabama	Teacher Education and Certification Section State Department of Education 349 State Office Building Montgomery 36130-3901	205/261-5060
Alaska	Coordinator of Teacher Education and Certification State Department of Education P.O. Box F, Alaska Office Building Juneau 99811	907/465-2810
Arizona	Arizona Department of Education Teacher Certification Unit 1535 West Jefferson P.O. Box 25609 Phoenix 85007	602/542-4367
Arkansas	Teacher Certification Room 106-107-B Arkansas Department of Education Little Rock 72201	501/371-1474
California	Commission on Teacher Credentialing 1812 9th Street Sacramento 94244-2700	916/445-7254
Colorado	Colorado Department of Education Teacher Certification 201 East Colfax Ave. Denver 80203	303/866-6628
Connecticut	Chief, Bureau of Certification and Accreditation State Department of Education P.O. Box 2219 Hartford 06145	203/566-4561

Table 5. *(continued)*
State Teacher Certification Offices

Delaware	Supervisor of Certification and Personnel Department of Public Instruction Townsend Building Dover 19903	302/736-4688
District of Columbia	Director of Certification and Accreditation District of Columbia Public Schools, Room 1004, 415 12th Street, N.W. Washington, D.C. 20004-1994	202/724-4230
Florida	Administrator, Teacher Certification Department of Education Knott Building Tallahassee 32301	904/488-2317
Georgia	Director of Certification Georgia Department of Education 1452 Twin Towers East Atlanta 30334	404/656-2406
Hawaii	Administrator (Certification) Office of Personnel Services State Department of Education P.O. Box 2360 Honolulu 96804	808/548-5215
Idaho	Director of Teacher Education and Certification State Department of Education Len B. Jordan Office Building Boise 83720	208/334-3475
Illinois	Manager, Teacher Certification and Placement Illinois State Board of Education 100 North First Street Springfield 62777	217/782-2805
Indiana	Director, Div. of Teacher Certification Indiana Department of Education Room 229, State House Indianapolis 46204	317/269-9715

(continued)

Table 5. *(continued)*
State Teacher Certification Offices

Iowa	Director, Division of Teacher Education and Certification State Department of Public Instruction Grimes State Office Building Des Moines 50319	515/281-3245
Kansas	Director, Certification Section State Department of Education 120 East 10th Street Topeka 66612	913/296-2288
Kentucky	Director, Division of Teacher Education and Certification State Department of Education 18th Floor, Capitol Plaza Tower Frankfort 40601	502/564-4606
Louisiana	Director, Higher Education and Teacher Certification State Department of Education Baton Rouge 70804-9064	504/342-3490
Maine	Director, Teacher Certification and Placement Division of Certification, Placement and Teacher Education State House Station 23 Augusta 04333	207/289-5944
Maryland	Assistant Superintendent in Certification and Accreditation State Department of Education 200 West Baltimore Street Baltimore 21201-2595	301/333-2142
Massachusetts	Director, Bureau of Teacher Preparation, Certification and Placement Quincy Center Plaza 1385 Hancock Street Quincy 02169	617/770-7517
Michigan	Director, Division of Teacher Preparation and Certification Services State Department of Education P.O. Box 30008 Lansing 48909	517/373-1926

Table 5. *(continued)*
State Teacher Certification Offices

Minnesota	Manager, Personnel Licensing and Placement State Department of Education 616 Capitol Square Building 550 Cedar Street St. Paul 55101	612/296-2046
Mississippi	Supervisor of Teacher Certification State Department of Education P.O. Box 771 Jackson 39205	601/359-3483
Missouri	Director of Teacher Education and Certification State Department of Education Jefferson Building, 7th Floor P.O. Box 480 Jefferson City 65102	314/751-3486
Montana	Office of Public Instruction Certification Services State Capitol Helena 59620	406/444-3150
Nebraska	Director of Certification and Teacher Education State Department of Education 310 Centennial Mall South Box 94987 Lincoln 68509	402/471-2496
Nevada	Supervisor of Teacher Certification State Department of Education 400 West King Street Carson City 89710	702/885-3116
New Hampshire	Director of Teacher Education and Professional Standards State Department of Education 101 Pleasant Street Concord 03301-3860	603/271-2407
New Jersey	Director, Office of Teacher Certification and Academic Credentials State Department of Education 3535 Quakerbridge Road, CN 503 Trenton 08625-503	609/588-3100

(continued)

Table 5. *(continued)*
State Teacher Certification Offices

New Mexico	Certification Director Division of Teacher Education and Certification State Department of Education DeVargas and Don Gasper Street State Capitol Complex, Room 105 Santa Fe 87501-2786	505/827-6581
New York	Division of Teacher Certification Cultural Education Center Room 5A 11 Madison Avenue Albany 12230	518/474-3901
North Carolina	Director, Division of Certification State Department of Public Instruction 116 West Edenton Street Raleigh 27603-1712	919/733-4125
North Dakota	Director of Teacher Certification State Department of Public Instruction State Capitol, 9th Floor Bismarck 58505	701/224-2264
Ohio	Director, Division of Teacher Education and Certification State Department of Education Ohio Department Building, Room 1012 Columbus 43266-0308	614/466-3593
Oklahoma	Administrator, Teacher Certification State Department of Education Hodge Education Building 2500 North Lincoln Boulevard Oklahoma City, 73105-4599	405/521-3337
Oregon	Teacher Standards and Practices Commission 630 Center St. N.E., Suite 200 Salem 97310	503/378-3586
Pennsylvania	Bureau of Teacher Preparation and Certification Department of Education 333 Market Street, 3rd Floor Harrisburg 17126-0333	717/787-2967

Table 5. *(continued)*
State Teacher Certification Offices

Puerto Rico	Department of Education Teacher Certification Div. Box 759 Hato Rey 00919	809/753-1168
Rhode Island	Coordinator for Teacher Education, Certification and Placement State Department of Education Roger Williams Building 22 Hayes Street Providence 02908	401/277-2675
South Carolina	Director of Teacher Education and Certification State Department of Education 1015 Rutledge, Room 1004 Columbia 29201	803/734-8464
South Dakota	Director, Office of Teacher Education and Certification Division of Elementary and Secondary Education Kneip Office Building 700 Governor's Drive Pierre 57501	605/773-3553
Tennessee	Director, Teacher Education and Certification State Department of Education 125 Cordell Hull Building Nashville 37219	615/741-1644
Texas	Director, Division of Teacher Certification Texas Education Agency William B. Travis State Office Building 1701 North Congress Avenue Austin 78701-1494	512/463-8976
Utah	Supervisor of Teacher Certification Instruction and Support Section Utah State Office of Education 250 East 500 South Salt Lake City 84111	801/533-5965
Vermont	Director, Certification Division State Department of Education Montpelier 05602	802/828-2445

(continued)

Table 5. *(continued)*
State Teacher Certification Offices

Virginia	Office for Professional Dev. & Teacher Education Division of Teacher Education and Certification Department of Education Box 6Q, James Monroe Building Richmond 23216	804/225-2094
Washington	Director of Professional Certification Office of the Superintendent of Public Instruction Old Capitol Building Olympia 98504-3211	206/753-6773
West Virginia	Director, Office of General & Professional Education State Department of Education Capitol Complex, Room B-330 Bldg. 6 Charleston 25305	304/348-7010
Wisconsin	Administrator, Teacher Certification Bureau of Teacher Education and Certification State Department of Public Instruction 125 South Webster Street P.O. Box 7841 Madison 53707-7841	608/266-1027
Wyoming	Director, Certification and Licensing Unit State Department of Education Hathaway Building Cheyenne 82002-0050	307/777-6261
St. Thomas/ St. John District	District Director Educational Personnel Services Department of Education St. Thomas, Virgin Islands 00801	809/774-0100
St. Croix District	District Director Educational Personnel Services Department of Education #21, 22 & 23 Hospital Street St. Croix, Virgin Islands 00820	809/773-1095

SUBSTITUTING

For various reasons, some educators prefer substituting over a contract position. Those wanting a career in substituting see it as exciting, challenging, less stressful, and more flexible than a full-time position. Once educators get to know you and like you, you are asked to return many times to the same school. If you decide not to work at a certain school or with a particular grade level or class, then the choice is yours.

Many substitutes come to class with their bag of teaching goodies, develop friendship and rapport with the other teachers, enjoy the experience of seeing different schools, students, and environments—and would not consider teaching any other way. (Substitute wages are also continuing to rise.)

If you are interested in substituting, call each district and inquire about their hiring procedures. Most require a completed application form and a short, easy interview. Get a map of all the schools and find locations ahead of time. You can substitute in several districts. You can also state your preference for grade levels, days of the week, and schools. Of course, the more you limit yourself, the fewer jobs you will get.

Organize a notebook of ideas to take to each assignment—songs, books, games, activities, projects—as appropriate for your level and subject. If you are given lesson plans, follow them as closely as possible. Leave a positive note for the teacher at the end of the day. (There is nothing worse for the regular teachers than returning to school to a list of horrible things that happened in their absence.) Sign the note. Tell which assignments were completed. Leave students' work for the teacher to see. Always correct all students' work. Remember, teachers and principles do talk about substitutes. The word spreads fast on who to request again. Some never get an opportunity to return.

If you are substituting only until you get a full-time position, follow all the guidelines above, except do not spread yourself too thin. Limit yourself to two or three schools in the district of your choice and get to know everyone. Establish rapport with the educators, the secretary, and the support personnel. Inform others of your professional goals. Make a special effort to thank the principal at the end of the day.

Substituting is an effective way to get a positive reputation established and to make important contacts. Short-term substituting at the end of your student teaching assignment is an excellent way to get acquainted with the schools in the district of your choice, and also let them get to know you. Always do your best every day you substitute. A poor record of substituting severely limits your chances of being hired.

THE SEARCH—A LONELY JOB

During student teaching, beginners have a built-in network of friends. Active, committed, attending classes, and teaching at assigned schools, student teachers are busy, motivated, and involved. When the assignment ends, however, suddenly these new educators are thrust into a lonely waiting period. Time stretches out—time to wait out the uncertainty of whether or not they get their desired position and district. Many times applicants are not hired until school starts or even after school has started. Enrollment numbers, replacement needs, and sudden changes mean last minute assignments.

As time progresses and others begin receiving contract offers, depression can mount heavily. Former student teachers say this is the most stressful and depressing period for those who have not yet signed a contract. And it hits at the time an applicant most needs inner strength and self-confidence. Whether a beginner or veteran, there are things you can do to help alleviate this anxiety-producing waiting period.

First, stay in contact with your peers. This is when you need words of encouragement and understanding listeners. Use each other as a support system. As you proceed through the job search process, share new information and findings with each other.

This is also the time when a weekly plan of action becomes essential. Moping around and dwelling on feelings of anxiety and depression accomplishes nothing. Continue to gather information, make contacts, and follow up on all screening and hiring procedures. Continue to let employers know you are available and interested. This may be the time to enlarge geographical boundaries. Use all support systems available to help maintain a high level of energy and a positive mental state. Visit the college placement center often, talk with counselors, ask advice, and follow suggestions. Most of all, do not give up—even after school has started.

SUMMARY

Searching for a position is a personal investment of time, money, and energy. This chapter emphasized the importance of using all available resources and adhering to a strict plan of action. Planning and implementing an effective job search strategy is a complex and serious procedure.

The most critical area of your career search is yet to come—preparing for the interview. Chapter 4 provides guidance for self-presentation for your important sales meeting.

CHA4PTER

Interviewing
A Critical Task

The interview is a critical step in achieving your professional goal. From your sales brochures, the employer formed certain impressions of your abilities and qualities. If invited for an interview, you can be reassured that, on paper, your qualifications match their needs. Now, these impressions will be supported or negated in a twenty to forty minute face-to-face encounter. Using subjective evaluation, the interviewer attempts to determine if you truly are a special, challenged, and motivated person—the one who best fits the position, district, and community.

No two districts use the exact same hiring process. No two interviews are precisely alike. Yet, there are common elements and general principles governing all interviewing procedures. This chapter provides knowledge of these processes and it outlines the necessary steps for preparation and planning. Follow these guidelines with committed effort to build proficiency and self-confidence in the final stage of the career search process.

YOUR SALES OPPORTUNITY

What Is an Interview?

An interview is a structured and purposeful, two-way professional conversation. Unfortunately, many applicants see the interview from strictly a passive viewpoint. "Employers ask the questions, while I (feeling nervous and intimidated) try to impress them with my answers."

There is no doubt, during this professional business meeting, you are asked structured questions in an attempt to assess your fitness for the position. There is also no doubt, that you do most of the talking. (And this is necessary in order to market your skills, abilities, and personality.) However, it is also an opportunity for you to gather information. An interview should be a mutual exchange of dialogue—a two-way professional discussion. While they are assessing you, you are assessing them. An interview is the time you both decide if a professional match is possible.

Purpose of the Interview—Tasks to be Accomplished

Both you and the interviewer have two important tasks to accomplish in this crucial meeting.

As an applicant, your tasks involve taking an active role in presenting yourself as a true professional. Your first task is to sell yourself for the position. This is your one (and probably only) chance to personally communicate your special combination of skills, abilities, and personal experience. Like your tailored resume, interview responses are also custom designed. Good salesmanship depends on discovering the employer's needs, then highlighting your qualifications that are relevant for this particular position and district. Enter the interview situation ready to accomplish this task.

Your second, and equally important, task is to gather information. There are two reasons for this. Information helps uncover the employer's needs, which in turn gives you a chance to show how you can meet those needs. And, equally important, you gather information so you can intelligently make a decision if offered a contract. Is this the position, district, and community you really want? Does this career move match your most important values, needs, and goals? Is this where you will be happy, motivated, energetic, and productive?

Although gathering information for decision making is your responsibility, the interviewer is watching to see if you are accomplishing this task. The reason: Employers want to be reassured that you know who you are and what you want. They want to be convinced you can intelligently say, "Yes, I fit," if an offer is made. An important part of the process, therefore, is when the interviewer gives you a chance to ask questions. Allowing time for inquiries is not merely an act of courtesy. What you ask is assessed as an important part of your interview evaluation. "Do you have any questions?" can be interpreted as "Applicant, show me you've done your homework. Ask thoughtful, relevant questions. Convince me you are genuinely interested in this position and intelligent enough to have familiarized yourself with the district and the community. The last thing I need is an unhappy educator—one who doesn't fit. Prove to me you know what you want."

Asking relevant questions, then, plays an important part in selling yourself for the position. To paraphrase Voltaire, "Judge people by their questions rather than by their answers."

Interviewers also have two tasks to accomplish during this brief meeting. First, they determine if the applicant's background, experience, training, and education match the district's needs. (In reality, this data was assessed in the paper screening process.) Many times applicants expect the interview to be focused on facts regarding their degree, certification, college work, or field work assignment. A question or two may be asked to verify your documents or training, but basically, in reaching this final meeting stage, you have already passed that test.

The heart of the interview is the second and most important task. Seventy-five percent to 85 percent of the interview emphasis is focused on subjectively evaluating you as a unique special human being: Who you are, what you want to do and why; and determining if your personal attributes and values match the position, school district, and community.

Like evaluating your resume, this task is accomplished through personal assessment, subjective judgment, and intuition. However, this time the product of evaluation is you—up close and personal. The interviewer appraises those characteristics and qualities that cannot (no matter how creative your sales brochures are) be fully detected in paperwork.

All characteristics of the applicant are quickly assessed—appearance, character, motivation, communication and human relation skills, intelligence, enthusiasm, dependability, integrity, ability to motivate, professionalism, attitude, potential, and personality (and accomplished in less than an hour). This task cannot be completed if an applicant answers questions simply, yes or no. Understand that the interviewer's second task is the most significant one. Open up, share, inform, and communicate—or there is little for anyone to assess.

Many times, people tend to hold back, inhibited and embarrassed by what sounds like bragging. No one wants to appear aggressive or egotistical. The idea of selling ourselves is equally distasteful. However, in order to get the interviewer to respect and appreciate your special abilities, creativity, and talents, you should risk revealing who you are. Allow the employer to evaluate you.

Another mistake is answering, "Oh, it's all right here in my resume." If you attempt to rely on a piece of paper to communicate your attributes, you have missed the whole point of this meeting. Your marketing tools have accomplished the job of selling you for an interview. Paperwork will not sell you in the interview. It is up to you now. During this crucial business meeting, use your resume only as mental framework. Expand on it with effective, convincing, oral communication.

The important "Tasks to Be Accomplished" are a shared duty. Both you and the interviewers have equal responsibility in making sure they are completed. Hiring officials help you accomplish your two tasks. You are given the opportunity to sell yourself and gather the information you need. It is your job to assist the interviewers in completing their two tasks. If the right questions are not asked to get a good picture of you, you will not get a job offer. It is in your best interests to help make sure the interviewers get the right information they need.

Interview Structures: Formats and Styles

Although many applicants look upon the hiring procedure as an obscure, mysterious, or even random process, districts follow well-defined guidelines in selecting educators.

Hiring processes consist of several different interview formats:

One to one—you and one interviewer.
A panel—you and several interviewers.
Multiple interviews—a series of meetings with individuals or groups.

In some districts one person does all the interviewing. Others use an interviewing team—individually meeting with applicants or assembled to record responses. As part of the interview, teachers are sometimes asked to prepare a short lesson, then teach the lesson to a group of students provided by the district. Administrators usually have an interview with the school board. Universities many times use a search committee. Most school systems today require at least two interviews: an initial screening, followed by a meeting with a principal, department head, or superintendent. You may be interviewed by a teacher selection committee, or by the entire faculty. Any and all combinations of the above may be used.

Interview styles also differ widely. These variations are based on the personality, expertise, and needs of the interviewer(s), and the particular school district's policy. Styles vary anywhere on a continuum—from the seemingly casual, informal approach to a very structured, intense, and even threatening procedure.

Many employers see interviewing as a tiring, time-consuming, but extremely important task. The interviewer is pressured to gather specific information in order to make a critical decision in a very short time.

Interviewers are often quite adept at altering their manner, voice, questioning, and apparent friendliness as they attempt to gather information needed to make a decision. A seemingly informal, almost casual conversation may suddenly change with an overtly pointed test question. Part of the interviewer's job is to observe your response in a pressure situation and to discover your level of confidence. This is why it is important to go into an interview knowing what you want the employer to *learn about you*, with solid understanding of your special qualities and strengths, and with knowledge of what *you* want. Then, whatever question is asked, in whatever manner, you will be able to respond with integrity, sincerity, and self-confidence.

In a discussion of interview styles, it is important to mention a commonly used method, the SRI Teacher Perceiver Interview. It is a copyrighted interview developed by Selection Research Incorporated, a Lincoln, Nebraska firm. This instrument was developed in an attempt to create an impartial, consistent, and objective interview process.

After a brief introduction, the applicant is asked to respond to a set of questions. The method is a planned situation, rigid, and uniformly structured. Answers are recorded (either written or actually taped), and graded on a standard. Specialists trained in the Perceiver Interview Method are neutral, unbiased, and accepting. They are trained not to reflect approval or disapproval of a candidate's response. Very possibly there is no interchange of information or ideas (zero feedback) between the applicant and the one listening.

Many employers are comfortable with the SRI approach, believing it gives them an objective means of equally evaluating all applicants. Many applicants are uncomfortable with the SRI approach, believing it to be a cold, unfeeling event, accompanied by detached and indifferent interviewers.

The questions used in this objective technique are based on real-life subjective situations. Applicants are often asked to respond to a given set of circumstances, e.g., "What would you do if...." The intention of this analytical instrument is to pinpoint applicants who exhibit a humanistic approach to education. Desired responses reflect brief, yet complete information demonstrating the following about the applicant:

- Sensitivity to and genuine interest in the needs of the individual student.
- Motivation to provide a stimulating, exciting learning environment that enhances the achievement and self-esteem of each individual.
- Realization and appreciation for the importance of each human being, and a true belief that every student counts.

Although many districts use this method (or a similiar one based on the SRI approach), it is usually combined with other types of interviews. Being aware of this technique, its intended purpose, and the *motivation for its usage*, helps you put it into proper perspective. It is merely another interview technique.

In summary, there are a multitude of interview structures with diverse formats and styles. Expect and be prepared for anything and everything. Interviewing, regardless of the procedure or technique, is stressful. Anxiety can be reduced by doing your homework. Read school literature. Talk to others who are interviewing. Meet with educators working in your desired districts (preferably recently hired ones). Visit schools. Discuss information with your career center counselors. You may be able to discover what interview styles, methods, and hiring practices are used. Gathering information for the purpose of becoming informed and prepared is your best defense against surprises. The bottom line is that when you are truly prepared—with inner knowledge of who you are, what you want, what you have to offer, and what you need to find out—the interview structure itself really makes no difference.

Elements of an Interview

Although interviews vary, each one usually contains four basic elements.

1. *Introduction.* On the surface, this stage seems little more than a simple exchange between two people who have just met. However, do not underestimate the significance of a positive beginning. Like the opening lines of a speech, first impressions are extremely important.

    Within the first four minutes, the employer has formed certain beliefs based on your appearance and initial presentation. Therefore, your sales strategy begins the moment you walk in the door. Appearance, voice, the way you walk, talk, sit, shake hands, and all verbal and nonverbal communication are a reflection of your professional image. The whole package you present is subjectively evaluated.

    It is important to practice making a favorable entrance. You never have a second chance to make a first impression. Rehearse in front of a mirror and with another person. Have a natural smile, a firm hand shake, good eye-contact, and an assertive beginning. "Hello, Dr. Grant, it's nice to meet you, my name is Erin Salzman." It does not take long for a trained and experienced interviewer to determine from your appearance and manner if you know who you are and what you have to offer.

2. *Background and Discussion.* Generally after the introduction, you are briefly asked about your background. These will be why, where, and when questions regarding your education, certification, experience, and interests. Your answers provide valuable insight for the interviewer. While you give details regarding your preparation and qualifications, the interviewer is connecting what you say with how you say it. Important qualities are measured in this beginning process of determining who you are.

3. *Matching you with the Position, the District, and the Community.* As the interview progresses, the employer puts together more pieces of the puzzle—forming an image of you as a professional and as a unique human being.

   Impressions develop from a combination of your initial presentation, background, personality, self-confidence, ease in relating to others, and facility in communicating in a clear and logical manner. Conclusions are made regarding your enthusiasm, motivation, emotional stability, overall human relation skills, sincerity, maturity, potential—and how the total you matches their needs.

   At this point the interviewer may also discuss the district's policies and expectations of their employees and sell the district to you. This is vital information, since it provides clues to what they need and want.

4. *Asking Questions and Conclusion.* Near the end of the interview, you have a chance to ask questions or volunteer additional information. Take advantage of the opportunity to present qualifications or abilities not brought out or discussed, particularly areas where you can fill their needs. (See p. 117 for primary and secondary needs.)

   This is also the time to get the answers required to make your decision—"Is this the right position for me?" Your questions tell a great deal about you. It is better not to ask questions than to ask inappropriate ones, such as "How much does this position pay?" An inquiry like this shows you did not prepare—you are not aware educators' salaries are public information—and your primary interest is the paycheck, rather than the special aspects of this position.

   Appropriate questions confirm that you have done your homework. You have learned about the district, considered how you might fill a need, and thought carefully about additional information needed to make a career decision. You may want to confirm facts gathered while researching the position. You may want to inquire about current or anticipated employment opportunities. Time is limited, therefore selectively choose one to three well thought-out questions. This chapter provides sample questions for your consideration.

   It is possible after doing your homework, researching the position, and completing student teaching or other experience in the district that you have found your answers and have made a decision. Tell the interviewer what you know.

Example

> "Dr. Grant, I've read the literature on your district and I've re-searched this position. I've lived in the community for five years and have completed two semesters of student teaching here. I feel from the information I've gathered and the experiences I've had that Glendale School District is a good fit for me. My teaching methods match your educational philosophy, and the high school position you told me about is the challenge I've been looking for."

Lasting impressions are as important as first impressions. When the interview is over, never try to prolong it. But, do prepare a concluding remark clearly communicating two things:

1. You are still interested in the position (if you truly are).
2. You appreciate their time and consideration. (Also inquire about what happens next if the interviewer has not already given this information.)

Example

> "After talking with you today, Dr. Grant, I'm more interested than ever in this third grade position. What are the next steps in the hiring procedure?"
> Or "When can I expect to hear from you?"

Never take notes during the interview. However, writing information or directions at the end of the interview shows you are organized and prepared. Have a small notebook and pen available. It is also acceptable to refer to some previously written questions noted while researching the position, or to refer to notes for important information you need to communicate.

Exit with a warm hand shake, a smile, and a positive message:

> "Dr. Grant, thank you so much for your time and consideration. I'm very interested in this eighth grade math position, and feel I'd make a strong contribution to the Glendale School District. I look forward to hearing from you."

Your final words confirm you are eager, ready, and willing to take on the responsibilities of this new position.

Interviewer Needs

In addition to finding a candidate to fill the specific requirements of a position (grade, subject, particular expertise), interviewers also look for certain qualities in their educators. These represent the employer's needs. Applicants who hear the needs of the interviewer and relate positively to them greatly increase their chances of being offered a contract. This is accomplished by listening for clues offered and communicating how your attributes, experience, and achievements fill those needs.

Interviewers' needs fall into two categories: presentation needs and professional needs. They are communicated as either primary (expressed) or secondary (implied) needs.

Presentation Needs

Presentation needs are qualities that are essentially a part of you, the person, rather than you, the educator. The interviewer draws conclusions about your character from insights gathered from the way you speak, how you conduct yourself, your manner, and your total presentation. Table 6 lists areas to consider.

Your actions (the manner in which you communicate these presentation needs) are a direct result of your attitude. Therefore, it is important to take time to assess your attitude. How do you see yourself fitting into this position? What are your beliefs, feelings, philosophy and outlook regarding this district and community? What expectations do you have?

The way you present yourself—your appearance, posture, manner, voice, all communication, even the expression on your face—is a reflection of your attitude. Do not try to fake it in an attempt to impress the interviewer. When a candidate tries too hard, smiles too much, or overperforms to make a positive impression, the interviewer becomes uncomfortable. The best advice we can offer in meeting these presentation needs is to present yourself as a self-confident, energetic, and convincing person. Be yourself...but at your best.

If you are genuinely interested in this position and district, pleased to get the opportunity to interview, and ready to accomplish the necessary tasks—you will impress them. Being prepared enhances a positive attitude, which in turn strengthens your self-confidence. Self-confident people show natural enthusiasm and authenticity.

Let your real professional self show through.

Table 6.
Presentation Needs

APPEARANCE	Your overall professional look—appropriate dress, posture, personal hygiene, neatness and grooming.
BODY LANGUAGE	Eye-contact, level of interest, attention and attentiveness, listening skills, poise.
HUMAN RELATION SKILLS	Likability, friendliness, pleasantness and sociability, flexibility, natural smile, sincerity and rapport.
VOICE	Clear, pleasant, well-modulated, and distinct speech.
LANGUAGE	Well-developed professional vocabulary, good grammar, well-formed sentences, no street jargon ("...ya know, kids are...," "...I really like art and all that creative stuff...").
THINKING SKILLS	Quick grasp of the meaning of questions asked, understanding and perception of ideas presented, easy comprehension of both obvious and subtle points, logical organization in presenting ideas.
PERSONAL ENTHUSIASM	Motivation, involvement, energy level, eagerness without giddiness, dedication and commitment, initiative, positive attitude.
SELF-CONFIDENCE	Composure, confident of abilities without being cocky or arrogant, emotional balance (can handle a stressful situation), well-prepared, comfortable, self-assured, secure, in control.

Professional Needs

Professional needs are qualities that are essentially the part of you as an educator. Interview questions dealing with professional needs are designed to give the employer an overall picture of your abilities, potential, and level of proficiency in your career field.

When answering questions based on professional needs, demonstrate understanding and mastery of these qualities by stating specific examples of application, your expertise, and accomplishments.

Remember, your past is an indication of your future potential. Whether it is twenty years experience or a few months of student teaching, review how you put these textbook ideas and concepts into everyday practice. How do you motivate your students? What classroom management system do you use, and how exactly do you apply it? How do you reinforce rules? How do you prepare a lesson? How exactly do you get parents involved in the learning process? What are the positive results of your committed efforts? Practice out loud presenting concise, enthusiastic and comprehensive answers. Use active positive phrases and give specific examples:

"I maintained an optimal learning environment by organizing cooperative learning groups to enhance..."

"I motivated students by creating a math center that increased...."

"I created a positive classroom environment, with fair, firm standards by...."

"One example of how I effectively involved parents in the learning process was...."

"I met the needs of each individual student by designing learning centers to...."

"One way I integrated subjects was...."

"During science, I stimulate active participation by...."

"One very successful method I used to keep track of individual skill development was...."

"I strengthened cultural awareness by designing and implementing a unit...."

"At the Mathematics National Convention in September, I learned a new method of teaching beginning geometry concepts...."

Stating specific examples (with results) show you understand and recognize the importance of this professional need and successfully incorporate it into your professional working day.

Table 7 lists professional needs. For each area, practice stating specific examples of how you achieve success.

Table 7.
Professional Needs

ENTHUSIASM FOR EDUCATION AND FOR STUDENTS
   Motivation, involvement, energy, willingness to learn and progress, eagerness, commitment and dedication to students and learning, history of working with and being involved in activities related to career, special skills, talents, or training, interest in extracurricular activities.

INTERPERSONAL RELATIONSHIPS
   Willingness to cooperate and contribute as a team player, human relationship skills with students, parents, fellow workers, principal and/or department head, and staff.

SOCIAL AWARENESS
   Awareness of contemporary issues, community involvement, personal activities as related to profession, sensitivity to cultural differences.

PROFESSIONAL AWARENESS
   Knowledge and awareness of latest developments in subject/grade level, knowledge of the field of education in general, familiarity with professional literature, sound philosophy of education that matches the district or college.

EDUCATOR'S COMPETENCIES
   Ability to Educate and Motivate:
      Knowledge and abilities in subject(s) and grade area.
      Teaching (or managing) techniques.
      Motivational learning techniques (with class in general and with specific individuals).
      Maintaining classroom control.
      Management of classroom (or school) environment.
      Use class time effectively and productively.
      Communication skills.
      Relating curriculum to students' needs.
      Maximize the learning potential of all students.
      Leadership ability.
      Flexibility and patience.
      Ability to analyze situations.
      Maintain a positive approach to educating.
      Creative abilities.
      Managing stressful situations.
      Organizational ability.
      Teaching critical thinking skills.
      Effective use of questioning strategies.
      Establish and maintain high consistent standards for achievement.
      Integrating skills and concepts into several subjects.

Table 7. *(continued)*
Professional Needs

Ability to Plan:
    Objectives specified.
    Long-term, short-term planning.
    Definite purpose in plans.
    Motivation technique stated in lesson design.
    Logical progression in planning.
    Practical systematic approach to planning.
    Meeting deadlines in planning.
    Knowledge of each step in a lesson design approach
Ability to Assess Student Progress:
    Evaluation techniques and procedures.
    Record keeping.
    Diagnosing for instruction.
    Recognition of individual learning and behavioral problems.
Ability to Relate to Students and Adults:
    Understanding student development.
    Recognizing student needs.
    Providing for individual and group differences.
    Human relationship skills with adults.
    Working with varying abilities and ages.
    Working with students of different cultural backgrounds.
    Development of self-esteem along with learning.
    Solving difficult communication problems.

Although all the qualities and abilities listed in Table 7 are desired in educators, certain characteristics and skills are crucial, based on the particular needs of the position and district. The following section describes how these needs are communicated.

Primary and Secondary Needs

When interviewers ask a question or make a statement, many times they are communicating one or more of the presentation or professional needs mentioned above. These are communicated as either primary needs (expressed) or secondary needs (implied). A primary need is easily identified as the one the interviewer is addressing at the moment. Secondary needs are ones inferred from the interviewer's questions and comments.

Expressed needs may be related to specific requirements of the job or they may describe special desired personal qualities. You can relate positively to these needs by directly connecting it with a quality of your own (using specific examples of success), or by demonstrating a desirable attitude of willingness towards it.

Example

> *Interviewer*: "In our upper grades, we have some problems. Many students are reading below grade level."
> *Applicant*: "I understand your concern. During my student teaching assignment we also had sixth graders reading below grade level. One technique we used with success was a literature-based reading program taken from the University of Portland's Read for Success Project. We informed the parents of this new approach, and they also became involved in the program. My supervising teacher and I were thrilled with the students' interest and their improvement in reading competencies."

Employers' needs sometimes appear in the form of objections, disapproval, or questioning of your abilities or qualifications.

Look critically at your experience, age, where you grew up, and your training, and predict possible objections to your qualifications. The reason there may be objections to your qualifications is not because they necessarily want to eliminate you from the competition. (If so, you would have been screened out during the paperwork process, and not even be in the interview.) The technique of questioning in the form of objections is used to express a need ("...applicant, convince me you can help solve my problem"), and/or to evaluate your level of confidence ("...applicant, convince me you can handle this position").

Example

> *Interviewer*: "We like to hire principals who have more experience."
> *Applicant*: "I realize other applicants may have more experience, but I feel the quality of my experience is what counts. I've had _____ years of professional experience in the areas of _____. My special training concentrated on _____. I used a new leadership technique from the _____ seminar when I directed the _____ committee last year. Dr. Russell said the results from our successful work led to _____. I have strong leadership abilities. I combine this with dedicated work and commitment to whatever I take on. I am a very enthusiastic leader and feel I can do an outstanding job in the Woodland District."

If your qualifications are questioned, clearly communicate your special abilities and accomplishments in terms of your suitability to the position. Then demonstrate your willingness, confidence, potential, and enthusiasm to get the job done.

The following are need statements an interviewer might communicate. Change the wording to make them applicable to your situation and try formulating responses based on your experiences.

"We've been working to improve our reading and math national test scores."

"We're looking for educators who involve parents in the learning process."

"I see that you haven't had any exposure to team teaching."

"We're a close working faculty and believe in an open classroom approach."

"The last few years we've had an increasing discipline problem in the seventh and eighth grades."

"You haven't had much experience. Do you think you can control thirty thirteen-year olds?"

"We have a multicultural, bilingual student population here."

"We'd prefer a teacher who speaks a second language."

"We have many older instructors in this district."

"Sophomores seem to lose interest after the first quarter."

"We think we may have combination classes next year."

"We're looking for a college instructor with graduate teaching experience."

"We like to have our teachers take full advantage of our new multimedia center."

"We're using the newest math teaching methods."

"We want professors who stay current in their fields."

"We believe in a humanistic philosophy of education."

"I notice you have a degree in art. We place strong emphasis on the basics."

"We feel our principals should involve themselves in community activities."

"Our last high school principal had outstanding rapport with the parents."

Many times a need is expressed, and you are given a chance to respond. Often, however, clues are offered while the interviewer is talking about other things. Keep these needs in mind and refer to them later.

Example

Interviewer: "As you may know, we are looking for a teacher for a fourth grade opening. This is a team-teaching situation in a multicultural area. The current teacher, Mrs. Whitman, is taking a year's leave. I notice you haven't had any fourth grade experience."

Respond first to the final statement (no fourth grade experience), and make a mental note of the other needs, team teacher and multicultural.

Applicant: "That's true. I haven't had any direct experience in fourth grade. However, I've taught at the second and fifth grade levels during my student teaching experiences, and was an aide for a year in a third grade class. I met with Mrs. Whitman last week and spent the morning in her classroom. I feel my background, education, and personal motivation will make me a strong educator with these fourth graders. By the way, you may have noticed from my resume, that my fifth grade placement was in a multicultural, bilingual area. One of my special projects was developing a social studies unit based on our students' diverse cultural backgrounds. We invited the parents for a final drama and musical presentation. My supervising teacher and I felt it was a very successful project. I feel I would make a positive contribution working in a multicultural environment."

The applicant responded positively to the grade level requirement, showed interest in and knowledge of the position, then related to the need for a multicultural teacher. This applicant chose to store the reference to team teaching and refer to it later in the interview.

Example

"Dr. Grant, you mentioned earlier you were looking for a team teacher. I feel I would be a strong contributing team member. I believe in open communication and working together towards solutions. I'm very willing to work in a team teaching situation."

This candidate had no team teaching experience, yet the statement tells the interviewer the message was heard and a willingness to fill the need is demonstrated.

An employer's needs can be used in formulating questions.

Example

"Dr. Grant, you mentioned earlier you were looking for a strong team teacher. I'm curious to know how your team teaching curriculum works. Would you please explain your program for me?"

In conclusion, always share an interest in the employer's problems and needs and demonstrate the desire to assist in meeting those needs. You do this by:

1. Researching the position, then tailoring your answers to match gathered information.
2. Asking questions to uncover needs, then demonstrating how you can solve their problems.
3. Listening for areas of need in the employer's statements and questions and reacting to them with specific examples of accomplishments.

Hearing and responding to the interviewer's needs is a crucial part of selling yourself. The most powerful message you can communicate during the interview is "I understand your needs and I have the confidence, knowledge, and commitment to meet those needs."

Building Self-Confidence

A television commercial says it clearly, "Being nervous is natural. Looking nervous is deadly." Every applicant who is aware of the importance of this crucial meeting is nervous. In less than an hour you are expected to radiate enthusiasm, poise, and the professional knowledge and know-how to convince the employer that you (of the hundreds of candidates) are the right choice. No matter who you are, or what position you are seeking, it can be a frightening event.

The good news is that reducing anxiety, building self-confidence, and looking and responding in a poised and confident manner is possible. Like all things worthwhile, it involves hard work. Some candidates make the mistake of thinking once an interview is scheduled, the work is over. In reality, once an interview is scheduled, your work begins. No one has innate superior abilities in interviewing—it is a learned skill. The formula is planning, practice, and preparation.

To build self-confidence, a candidate must prepare as if studying for an important final exam. Assuming everyone cares about doing well, two distinct groups enter a testing situation. One group displays obvious nervousness. They are jittery and high-strung with tense mannerisms. The other presents a more self-confident image—composed, poised, and controlled.

The difference between the groups is readiness. The latter group is prepared. They did their homework. They attended every class, asked questions, finished all assignments, studied their notes and text, researched information, joined a study group, and planned time to thoroughly review all materials. Having a good night's sleep and adequate nutrition, they enter the testing situation alert and ready. They know they did all they could do and will do the best they can.

It does not mean they have eliminated all stress. In fact, researchers show moderate levels of stress actually can increase one's alertness and performance. The group members who are prepared, however, feel that they are in-control—and consequently their nervousness is under control. Knowing they are prepared, their self-confidence is strengthened. They are anxious and ready to complete the necessary tasks.

The other group did no homework. They missed classes, finished few assignments (if any), did no research, asked no questions, made no effort to discuss ideas with others, and had nothing to review. Not only did they not study the textbook, they did not even buy one. Muddled attempts to study, along with a severe onset of test anxiety, began late the previous night (after an important party). Entering the testing situation, they are fatigued, dull, fearful, and extremely anxious. They have good reason to be nervous. They know they are unprepared and will probably fail.

External and Internal Readiness

Planning, practice, and preparation to strengthen your interviewing skills and build self-confidence involve two related aspects—external readiness and internal readiness.

The focus of external readiness is what you do outwardly—gather, organize, plan, study, analyze, investigate, research, examine, observe, and rehearse.

Before the interview, review all information gathered while conducting your market research. Study district literature. If you have not done so already, call and visit recently hired educators or people you know in the district. Check your college placement office, local Chamber of Commerce, and library for district information. Read community newspapers. The more you know about the district, its policies, and philosophy of education, the less intimidating the interview.

Reanalyze and update your answers on the self-assessment questionnaire (chapter 1), as related to this particular district of interest. Re-evaluate how this position matches you.

Review your resume and cover letter. Plan your clothing and organize materials. Formulate appropriate questions to ask. Role play with a friend. Be the interviewer, as well as the applicant, to get insight into both roles. Your college career office may be able to assist you with interview guidance. Tape record or videotape your responses. Critique your answers, voice, and manner. This chapter includes a list of sample interview questions for practice.

The focus of internal readiness is psychological or inner preparation. It involves reflecting, appraising, speculating, and considering. This readiness is directed toward internal thoughts, feelings, attitudes, perspectives, and self-assessment.

A key ingredient for internal readiness is maintaining a positive attitude. One way of enhancing one's mental outlook is a technique called visualization. This popular method is used by athletes in training. Take time everyday to consciously visualize meeting the interviewer, feeling poised and prepared, answering questions with confidence, and handling the entire interview with mastery. Preparing for success in your mind helps improve your performance and confidence.

Sharing your successes and disappointments with someone you trust is equally essential for emotional balance. A confidant can give you the needed boost and support at times of distress and disappointment.

Our bodies and minds are greatly affected by what we eat, the amount of sleep we get, exercise, and leisure activities. Do not neglect your physical state of being.

Having a positive attitude means keeping things in perspective. No matter how diligently you prepare, some interviews are disappointing and frustrating. Let's face it—there are areas of the hiring process and specific employers' needs over which we have no control. Every interview (especially the most frustrating one) is an opportunity to gain self-knowledge. Moving forward means learning and growing from all experiences (and past mistakes). That is just what educators teach.

There is a direct correlation between external and internal readiness. The more you prepare outwardly (external readiness) the more confident you feel internally. When totally involved and focused on external preparation, thoughts are diverted from yourself. Instead of concentrating on feelings of anxiety, you focus on the current task of gaining important knowledge. Like preparing for the final exam, when truly concentrating on the assignment, apprehension diminishes.

Use the same principle during the interview. Concentrate on what the hiring official is saying, not on how they are perceiving you. Think through your answers, instead of focusing on the outcome of the meeting.

Remember, a certain amount of stress is expected. Anxiety is part of the process. After all, this meeting could lead to an important transitional period in your career and change the pattern of your life.

Channel stress into positive activities. Make it work for you by doing the following:

- Thoroughly plan, practice, and prepare.
- Continually update self-knowledge.
- Persevere and maintain a positive attitude.
- Keep a balanced state of being—physically, mentally, and emotionally.

Confidence, poise, and trust in one's own abilities come from inner knowledge, from the awareness and understanding that "I am prepared."

"I have done my homework. Beginning with self-assessment, I have really thought through who I am, what I want, and where I fit. I know how I feel about myself as a professional."

"I've completed all the necessary steps. I've developed good sales brochures. (They got me this interview.) I've gathered information on this position, district, and community. I have a few questions which need to be answered. I'll use this opportunity to get the information I need. If offered a contract, I am ready (or nearly ready) to make a decision."

"I feel I look good. I'm well rested and dressed appropriately, which gives me confidence. I understand why I'm here, what I have to do, and the importance of completing all tasks."

"I am ready to sell my qualities. I've practiced answers to possible interview questions. I'll enter with a positive attitude, a smile, a firm handshake, and a calm, poised approach."

"I am a well-trained, capable professional. And I'm ready to let others discover and appreciate my special qualities. I will do my best. And, because I am prepared, my quiet confidence will come through loud and clear."

Interview Guidelines

1. *Be on time.* Arriving late severely hurts your chances of being hired. (Five minutes after the arranged time is late.) The employer sees a late applicant as unreliable, unorganized and lacking consideration; and you begin this crucial meeting with an explanation and an apology. Some interviewing experts say it is best to call and cancel the appointment if you are going to be late.

    The best strategy is to plan ahead. Arrive twenty to thirty minutes early. This allows for heavy traffic and parking. If you are not sure of the location, it is wise to make a dry run the day before. Once you have arrived, use the time to review your resume. Think through practiced responses and recall points you want to emphasize.

    Although all materials were sent to the district during the screening process, arrive at the interview with a folder containing copies of all documents (including your resume). Order several copies of official sealed transcripts for this purpose. With hundreds of applicants and possibly many people on a screening committee, paperwork can become misplaced. This practice is also a demonstration of your personal organization and preparation abilities.

    Find the restroom. Check your appearance. Give yourself a mental pep-talk, and do some deep breathing, relaxation exercises. Five minutes before the scheduled time, introduce yourself to the receptionist. Ask if you can leave your coat or other parcels outside the interview room. Do not take anything with you except a briefcase or purse.

    Be courteous, friendly, responsive, and businesslike to everyone you meet. Refer to the interviewer as Mr., Dr., Mrs., or Ms. Have a friendly smile and firm hand shake. Do not sit until invited.

2. *Look professional.* This is important. An educator is a visible member of the community. What you wear and how you look sends a message. Employers hire people who have a businesslike appearance.

    Wear professional looking career quality clothes. Dress as if you were giving a speech representing your school district at a national convention. This is a business meeting. Wear conservative colors and styles.

Women should wear a career dress or suit. Stay away from V-necks and sexy-looking apparel. (Jackets give one a feeling of authority. There are many soft jacket looks in women's wear.) Wear a basic pump shoe, closed toe and heel. Go easy on make-up, jewelry, and cologne. Men should wear a long sleeve shirt and tie, or coat and tie, depending on the grade level and district, polished shoes, and should have a conservative hair cut.

3. This guideline appears so obvious, and yet needs to be emphasized: *Listen to the questions and answer them.* If asked to give an example of a successful discipline technique, give an example. Although you may follow with a statement of why this technique is successful, do not wander into an extended verbal essay on discipline philosophies. If asked to give five words describing you as an educator, give five words. Do not explain in great detail how you arrived at these five words.

Do not try to impress the interviewer with a heavy theoretical approach. Show an understanding of educational theory combined with practical experience. Demonstrate the ability to apply your education and learning to real-life situations.

A question or two can be directed back to the interviewer. Use this technique sparingly.

Examples

Interviewer: "What are your feelings regarding homework?"
Applicant: "I've seen homework handled in many different ways depending on the grade level, abilities, and needs of the individual students. The specific circumstances would dictate the amount of homework I assign. May I ask, what is the homework philosophy in this district?"

Interviewer: "We have some discipline problems here. Can you handle them?"
Applicant: "Teaching could get boring if all students were perfect. I find that creating stimulating and motivating lessons greatly cuts down on discipline problems, and I feel confident I can handle any that arise. Could you tell me, what types of discipline problems are most current in this school district?"

Do not overuse the question-to-answer-a-question technique. Using it in an attempt to put the interviewer on the spot will not work to your advantage. But a sincere inquiry related to a question is perfectly acceptable. Remember, interviewers' questions are clues to their needs. You can store information for future use.

Example

Interviewer: "Do you have any questions?"
Applicant: "You asked earlier about homework. In connection with that, I would like to know what is the Glendale School District's policy on homework?"

4. *Be an active listener.* Never interrupt. Show genuine interest as the interviewer speaks. Demonstrate active involvement in the conversation. (This is done with eye-contact, facial expression, body language, and verbal response.) When responding to a committee or panel of interviewers, speak to everyone, not just the one asking the questions.
5. *If you do not know the answer to a question, say so.* "I've never been asked that question before, I need a few moments to think about it," or "I know I should be prepared to answer that question, but I'm not." If you do not *understand* the question, ask for clarification.
6. *Stress the positive. Never criticize—anyone, anything.* Remember, what you say is a reflection of your professional image. During research, if you uncover a district problem, refer to it in a positive manner.

Examples

Interviewer: "What do you know about our district?"
Applicant: "What I've seen in your district is impressive. Your math curriculum for college prep students is outstanding. And, I also noticed you have some of the same problems we had in the North Bay District (discipline, multicultural needs, low achievers). Although I have no magical solutions, I am familiar with the problem...." (show ability in solving problem by stating positive results from your efforts or willingness to work towards solutions).

Interviewer: "Did you notice some of our instructors are not up-to-date in their teaching methods?"

Applicant: "It's hard to tell about people until you really get to know them, but personally I enjoy attending workshops and staying current with new ideas."

Interviewer: "Did you have any problems during student teaching?" (In your former department? At your previous school? If it was great, say so. If not....)

Applicant: "I feel I gained much knowledge and insight during my student teaching assignment. I view every situation as a learning experience, and make the most of every opportunity to grow in all areas. My master teacher was particularly helpful in the area of...."

If asked to explain a past failure, give the circumstances without making excuses or laying blame. Respect for others and integrity are important personal qualities.

To stress the positive, emphasize what you have done, not what you have not done.

Example

Interviewer (To freshmen science instructor): "Have you had any experience working with juniors and seniors?"

Applicant: "I have had many experiences working with juniors and seniors. Although I haven't taught an entire classroom of senior high students, I have used seniors as tutors in my freshmen classes. I also very successfully directed the after-school science club which was entirely made up of juniors and seniors. I was also involved in my own teenagers' high school activities, and feel I have excellent rapport with that age. More than anything else, I have strong motivation to work with this age group. I like the idea that they are capable of handling more difficult concepts in science. I am very eager to teach higher level science activities and incorporate ideas I gained from the Hartford University Science In-Service last semester. I know I have the energy and dedication to do an outstanding job and thoroughly prepare these students for college level science courses."

(See also "Primary and Secondary Needs," p. 117 for responding to employers' objections.)

7. *Never answer a question with a "no" without adding a positive qualifying statement.*

Examples

Interviewer: "Have you used the Sherwood math method?"
Applicant: "No, we used the Harris method, but I learn quickly and I'm very interested in new teaching methods."

Interviewer: "Have you used calculators in your math class?"
Applicant: "No, I haven't. However, I feel calculators can be a motivating and useful tool, as long as students continue to learn facts, and not rely solely on the instrument...."

8. *Stress enthusiasm and potential without bragging.* Most questions have no right or wrong answers. So, do not pretend to be a know-it-all. Sprinkle your phrases with: "In my opinion...." "One of the ways to handle that situation would be...." "There are many effective means of teaching reading. One method I've used successfully is...."

    Beginning educators may want to cushion some accomplishments with "We...." (indicating "My supervising teacher and I").

    A good way to stress enthusiasm is to let your experience speak for itself. Note the two responses to the question, "How are you a good educator?"

    "I'm great! I love kids. I always do my best." Or,... "I feel I am an excellent educator. My master teachers and my university supervisor gave me excellent evaluations. My dedication and energy level is tops. I have great compassion for the individual student and do whatever is necessary to help each one achieve success. I also have a strong interest in trying new methods and ideas. For example, the last few weeks while working with a low math group, I incorporated hands-on activities and learning centers based on ideas from the Walter University Math Project. It was exciting seeing the students' interest and their progression in skills. My master teacher plans on continuing with the learning center approach next semester. I have a lot of enthusiasm for teaching. I really look forward to the challenge of having my own classroom."

    Another aspect of enthusiasm and potential this applicant presented was an interest in new ideas. These are things you have tried, ideas you read in professional literature, workshop or coursework concepts, suggestions from other educators and instructors, and ideas gained from professional associations and new research. Your underlying message is "I am a continual learner. Although I've learned a lot, I also have a lot to learn. I will continue to gain knowledge and be open to new ideas in my field."

To stress enthusiasm, practice stating specific accomplishments to sell your qualities. Communicate clearly what you do well and your willingness to learn. Be self-confident and secure, without bragging or exaggerating. Combine energy and enthusiasm, yet maintain professional poise. Be assertive, not aggressive, friendly, yet businesslike. Present yourself as a multitalented, multifaceted educator—one who contributes beyond the normal duties. Show how you will contribute not only to the school, but to the total district and community. Be yourself. Employers hire people they feel comfortable with—natural enthusiasm, sincerity, and honesty are hard to fake.

9. And through it all, remember, *employers look out for their own best interests*. Following are questions and concerns uppermost in the hiring official's mind during the interview:

    • What does this applicant have to offer?
    • Why is he/she interested in my district (and this position)?
    • How can this individual benefit and help me?
    • Will this person "fit" in my district (or school)?

What Can Screen You Out

The law prohibits discrimination based on race, age, sex, religion, place or origin of birth, handicap, or marital or parental status. Hiring officials are human beings, however, equipped with their own set of prejudices. There are inherent factors beyond our control (nationality, age, sex, race). Other factors are well within our control. Notice the ones over which we do have control:

Answers too lengthy—too many examples, non-stop talking.
Answers too brief—no examples, "yes" or "no" answers.
No questions—no interest in position.
Unprepared—knows nothing about position or district.
Poor grammar, voice, diction.
Smoking or gum chewing.
Poor eye contact.
Body language conflicts with words.
Bored (blasé), indifferent, lack of interest and enthusiasm.
Desperate—I'll take anything.
Too aggressive—overly confident, know-it-all.
Too timid—shy, won't speak up.

Obvious nervousness—fidgeting, lack of confidence and poise.

Lack of courtesy—ill-mannered, argumentative.

Unprofessional appearance, poor grooming or personal hygiene.

Negative attitude—criticizing former employers, fellow workers.

Poor beginning—limp handshake, late, poor posture, no attempt to establish rapport, too serious and solemn.

Weight—Teaching or managing is a vigorous job. Employers feel overweight people are unhealthy and lack energy. Losing weight will give you an extra edge on the interviewer's perception of you. It may also raise your level of confidence.

Age—Age is probably the single factor most often used for discrimination. If you feel your age is a problem, take note of how you can be in more control of this element:

Too young—(not experienced enough) Demonstrate your potential, energy, enthusiasm, fresh point of view, how teaching (or managing) lends itself to a young person, willingness to learn, open to new ideas, and how you've made the most of the experience you've had. Dress in a strictly professional, conservative manner, and radiate maturity.

Too old—(not enough energy, not open-minded) Demonstrate stability, mature judgment, dedication, reliability, and responsibility. Show you know the value of a good position, are not afraid to work, and have a history of success. Radiate energy, vitality, openness to new ideas, and a healthy body and mind.

Possible Interview Questions

The following are ten commonly asked questions and suggestions for answers:

1. *"Tell me about yourself."* This often-used statement totally baffles unprepared candidates. Do not begin with your childhood or a give a summary of your life. Begin where you are right now. Do not ramble. Practice a 2- to 3-minute presentation (possibly 5 minutes for experienced educators with numerous accomplishments) on your current training, experience, education, skills, background and special qualities, as they relate to the position. Be as specific as possible. It is also beneficial to include something about yourself personally. Although it is illegal for an interviewer to ask your marital status or information regarding the care of your children, these are areas of interest. Opening up, sharing, and giving the interviewer an immediate positive comfortable feeling about you is an important part of this response.

In the following example, the applicant begins with facts regarding education and experience, states accomplishments, gives some family information, proves she has knowledge of the district, and has considered how she might fit in. She ends with statements describing personal characteristics.

Example

Interviewer: "Tell me about yourself."

Applicant: "I'd be happy to. I just graduated from Northwest University with a major in English. I completed two semesters of student teaching in the Glendale School District, in Westwood County. During my second semester I organized a literature group which....(stress accomplishments). While completing my education, I worked as a high school aide in Riverview. This work experience convinced me I wanted to have a career in education. My husband and I recently moved to this area. He is currently employed with the.... company and is very supportive of my education and professional goals. I've done some research on this opening and I found that my abilities in .... would fit perfectly with your educational philosophy of.... I visited Mr. Woodman at Glendale High School. He told me the pilot English program being used this year is.... I used a similiar approach during my student teaching assignments. It was very effective. For example, one group I worked with.... I feel I would make a valuable contribution to your district. I place a high value on education, I'm very dependable, enjoy creating exciting activity-oriented lessons, and have great concern for the achievement of the individual student."

End with: "Is there anything else you'd like to know?"

Sometimes, the employer will pick up on something you said and ask for an explanation. (Make sure you are able to prove your statements.)

Example

Interviewer: "You mentioned you enjoy creating exciting activity-oriented lessons. Explain one such lesson for me."

Applicant: "I use many activity-oriented lessons. During my student teaching assignment, one lesson which particularly stands out was the time I divided the class into cooperative learning groups to emphasize the concept of.... The results were fantastic. Not only were these juniors truly motivated and involved, but their critical thinking skills significantly improved...."

2. *"Why do you want to work for our district?"* or *"Why should we hire you?"* or *"What can you do for this position?"* The employer is trying to find out if you just want a job, or are you really interested in this district and position. Now is the time to show you have done your homework. There are several effective ways to begin your response.

Examples

"I'm interested in the Westview School District and this junior high position because...."

"I'm completing my second semester of student teaching in the Westview School District, and I feel my teaching (or management) methods are a perfect match with your district's philosophy of education...."

"I've researched this position and talked with several employees in your district. I believe I have the qualities that would fit this sixth grade opening...."

Continue your opening statement with several short, hard-hitting, organized reasons to support it.

3. *"What are your strengths (or special abilities) and weaknesses (or areas you feel you need improvement)?"* On listing strengths, do not go overboard. Get to the point immediately with a few well-thought-out examples to support your statements. In other words, not only state your special abilities, but tell how you use these strengths to make a contribution.

Example

"I feel I am adept at locating students' needs. My supervising teacher commented on my ability to use student feedback to locate weaknesses and then plan lessons to strengthen skills. I'm also dependable. I had perfect attendance during student teaching. My creative abilities have always been a strong point for me, not just in the art and music area, but also in creating motivating learning centers and creative hands-on activities to enhance daily lessons. I believe I'm a strong team member and have good communication abilities with students and adults. I believe in working together to solve problems and enjoy involving parents in the learning process."

Be prepared for "What is your one greatest strength?" Again, begin with a brief statement and clearly stated examples.

Example

"I feel I have many strengths, but if I were to choose one, it is my ability to motivate students and to get them totally involved and interested in learning. For example, last year...." (Use specific examples of achievement.)

Weaknesses are more difficult to explain. Who wants to admit a weakness in an interviewing situation? Applicants are often advised to briefly present a limitation or fault in a favorable light, if possible.

Examples

"I do tend to become very involved in my work, to the extent of taking it home with me at the end of the day."

"I feel a sense of restlessness if my objectives are not completed within my timetable."

A weakness can also be related to lack of experience.

Example

"I suppose my weakness is I've never held a position exactly like this one" (at this grade level, as an administrator). "However, I feel confident I can handle this position based on my education, my personal motivation, and my excellent training during my internship...."

You can show how something could be a strength and a weakness.

Example

"I'm not good at doing the same things over and over in exactly the same way. I find I like variety. Although, perhaps that is a strength, because I find students also like variation in work activities."

4. *"What interests you most about this position?"* This is similiar to "Why do you want to work here?" Give a brief, truthful response to show you understand the position.

Example

"I will enjoy the challenge of working with graduate students. During my assistantship, I organized a study group for graduates and I feel I am aware of their needs...."

5. *"Where do you see yourself five years from now?" "What would you like to be doing five years from now?" "What are your future (professional) plans (goals)?"* Give a response indicating you expect to grow professionally in experience and expertise. Project yourself in terms of the district and the position. If you are applying for a teaching position, do not wander into goals of becoming a principal or administrator. This is a question you can answer in general terms.

Example

"I'm a growth-oriented person. I enjoy learning and practicing new professional techniques. I plan to attend workshops, take graduate classes, and be involved in my professional association. I want to be the best, or one of the best educators, at whatever grade level (or subject) I am working with at that time. I feel all other things in my life will fall into place when I am achieving success in my profession."

6. Questions beginning, *"What would you do if..."* are frequently used in interviews. Many times these are situations regarding curriculum, methods, student/adult relationships, professionalism and ethics, discipline and classroom control. The quality of your answer is not as important as your attitude in dealing with the question. Rushing in displays an "I know it all" attitude. Instead, cushion answers with, "One of the things I might consider would be...." Review the humanistic approach response from the SRI method in answering this type of question. Emphasize the needs of each individual student.

7. *"What are your interests, hobbies, and activities outside of work?"* The interviewer is trying to get a picture of the whole person. Integrate your personal life with work if possible, by stating active participation in professional affiliations, educational growth, and outside activities in your educational field. Be prepared to support your answers if necessary.

Example

Interviewer: "You say you enjoy participating in professional activities. What recent activity did you attend?"

Personal growth activities, sports, as well as civic and family activities, are also acceptable answers for an interests question.

Examples

"When I get the time, I like to play tennis. I take aerobic lessons each week. I plan to enroll in a conversational Spanish class this fall."

"This last year, my life has been centered on preparing for my career. With graduate work and my internship, I haven't had much time for outside activities. However, if we settle here in Colorado, my husband, two sons, and I will enjoy becoming involved in skiing and sledding." (This statement relates outside activities to the community and environment.)

8. *"How long would you plan to stay in this district?"* (or university? or grade level?) Your answer can be general.

Example

"As long as it is a positive experience for the students, myself, and the district. Everything I know about this district tells me it is an ideal fit. I hope to stay indefinitely."

9. *"What is your philosophy of education?"* This is not as difficult as it appears. By now, you have formed many general beliefs, outlooks, and personal views regarding teaching (or administration). As with "Tell me something about yourself," prepare a brief two to three minute summary of these beliefs. (Refer back to your self-assessment.) Use specific examples describing accomplishments resulting from your efforts. End with "I could continue, but I'm not sure how much time we have. Is there anything else you'd specifically like to know about my philosophy?"

10. *"Why should we hire you over all the other applicants?"* The interviewer is really saying, "How are you special?"

Example

Applicant: "I cannot speak for the other applicants, only for myself. With the knowledge I've gathered on your district, I feel my abilities in…. match this position perfectly. I bring many strengths and special talents to this position…" (use your list of strengths and special abilities from your self-assessment). End with some personal qualities. "I feel my enthusiasm for teaching, dedication to my students, and love of mathematics would make me a valuable asset to your staff."

The following is a continued list of questions. (Certainly not all are asked in any one interview.) Practice answering them in an organized and believable manner. For most, there are no concrete right or wrong answers. The way you respond (your level of confidence, sincerity, enthusiasm, open-mindedness, and honesty) is evaluated. Adapt the questions to your particular level and subject.

Background Questions

- What can I do for you today? ("I'm here to discuss the position of…")
- How have your past experiences prepared you for teaching? (Or for administrating?)
- What grade level do you prefer? (Unless you are set on a specific level, use the want to and willing to approach. "I prefer grades ten to twelve, but I'm very willing to consider other levels.")
- Describe your educational background. What are your educational goals? What was your favorite subject in college? Why?
- How would you describe your last principal? Department head? Master teacher?
- What five adjectives describe you? What five adjectives describe your teaching (or managing) style?
- How did you select your major? (If applicable, be ready to explain why you moved from an unrelated major into education.)
- What do you know about our district (or university)? What part of your background matches our goals? What new or different ideas would you bring to our district?
- Tell me about your student teaching experience (internship, past professional experience). What was most effective about you? What have you learned in your experiences? What kind of problems did you have?

If you had student teaching to do over again, what would you do differently?

- What were your three most important accomplishments during student teaching (your internship, your professional career)? What has been your most positive teaching (or managing) experience? Negative experience?
- How have you involved parents in the learning process? Describe how you would establish and maintain positive working relationships with parents.
- What curriculum materials have you developed?
- How have you used (or would you use) paid aides in your classroom?
- What books, concepts, or experiences have influenced you the most in your professional development?
- How have you contributed toward the development of the total school program in your current position?

Subject Area and Grade Level Questions

- What do you feel is your strongest subject (or teaching) area? What subject is most difficult for you?
- How would you teach reading in your classroom (math) (science)? Describe a typical lesson.
- What activities do you use with your independent workers during reading?
- What supplementary reading (or other subject) materials do you find most helpful? What resources do you use other than the basal text?
- What do you feel are the most important things students should learn at your grade level (in your classroom, subject area)?
- How do you motivate a group of slow readers?
- How do you use math manipulatives?
- Describe an ideal curriculum in your area of study.
- Discuss a critical issue in your subject area.
- How have you emphasized the development of basic skills? What skills do you feel are most important at this grade level (or subject)? What math series are you using? Reading series?
- Have you used calculators in your lessons (computers)?
- What should students have gained from having taken your course? Why is your field important for a student to study? How do you view your subject in relation to the total school curriculum?
- (Elementary) Can you handle instruction in physical education, art, and music?

- (Secondary) Can you handle three or more preparations at the secondary level?

Teaching Technique Questions—Motivational Skills

- There are times when you may have an extra five or ten minutes left at the end of the period. What types of sponge activities do you use to make the best use of this time?
- Define cooperative learning and give an example of how you have used it.
- How would you individualize instruction to meet the needs of all your students? Would individualized instruction be a part of your teaching day?
- Describe a teaching strategy you used to maximize the learning potential of all students.
- Share with me a recent learning experience you developed for your students and how you organized that experience to enhance each student's success.
- Describe a closure activity.
- What role does active-participation play in your teaching techniques? Describe an active participation technique you use so you know the students understand the concept.
- How do you motivate students? Name three effective ways to motivate students.
- What innovative ideas would you like to initiate in your classroom?
- What are some examples of your classroom creativity? What strategies would you use to aid students in developing creativity?
- What extracurricular activities would you be willing to supervise?
- How have you stressed the development of cognitive skills within your classes?
- What kind of relationship do you have with your students?
- How do you reinforce self-esteem in students?
- Describe your typical teaching style. What teaching techniques do you use?

Philosophy of Education Questions

- What would be your ideal educational philosophy of a school (district)? (Be careful with ideal or dream job questions. Select the parts of your ideal that could be fulfilled in this position.)
- What do you consider an ideal class size?
- What is your philosophy on homework?

- What are you looking for in a school? a university? a district?
- Would you rather teach the slow learner or the advanced learner? Why?
- What is your philosophy on team teaching? Are you willing to work in a team-teaching situation? an open classroom situation?
- What is your position on behavior modification? special education? learning centers? time-out discipline methods? competency-based instruction? use of cooperative learning groups? computers in the classroom? career education? sex education? open-space classrooms? individualized instruction?
- What is your philosophy on grading, report cards, classroom management?
- What are your practices in dealing with controversial subjects?
- What issues in education are of greatest concern to you? Why?
- Describe the role of the teacher (the principal, the student, the counselor) in the learning process.
- How do you personally feel students learn?
- What is the most satisfying aspect of teaching (or managing)? Least satisfying aspect?
- What is most important to you in a position?
- Why do you want a career in teaching (or administration)? Why do you think you will be a good educator?
- What prompted you to go into the field of education?
- What should schools do for students?
- What is the toughest aspect of teaching today? What are some of the greatest challenges of being an educator?
- What is your greatest concern when in a classroom, or when managing?
- Define a superior educator. Describe some of the characteristics of an outstanding educator.
- How would you change the public schools (universities) if you could make any changes you wished?
- What does teaching (managing) really involve?
- What do you like most about being an educator? Least?
- What motivates you?
- How do you cope with stress?
- What are your concerns and outlook for the future of public education?

Evaluation Questions

- How will you appraise your own teaching performance? How will you determine if your students are learning?

- What evaluation techniques do you use? Do you grade on ability or effort? Why?
- How do you feel about observations by supervisors?
- How would your students describe you? Your colleagues? Principal (or department head)?
- How do you communicate with parents about a student's progress?
- How would you discover your students' feelings regarding your class?

Classroom Organization/Lesson Planning Questions

- How is (was) your classroom organized?
- What type of learning environment do you try to create?
- If I visited your class, what could I expect to find? What would I see that would indicate your program is meeting the needs of each student?
- What kind of grouping do you think is best?
- Do you use homogeneous or heterogeneous grouping?
- How would you work with a mainstreamed learning handicapped student?
- Describe independent study projects your students have completed.
- How do you structure your class to achieve maximum benefit from teacher/student contact?
- How do you handle the different ability levels of students? Different cultural levels? The gifted? The educationally or culturally deprived? Limited English-speaking students? How would you help a student who is having difficulty?
- Are you well organized?
- Do you believe in detailed lesson plans? In lesson planning, how do you organize and prepare your material? How do you use lesson plans?
- Describe the specific components or steps of an effective lesson plan.
- Outline your approach for preparing a science unit.

Classroom Control/Management Questions

- What is your philosophy of discipline? What are your convictions regarding discipline?
- What classroom management system do you use?
- Explain the structure of your discipline plan. What rules do you establish in your classroom?
- How do you handle discipline problems?
- What is the toughest aspect of discipline?

- How would you handle a student who is a consistent behavioral problem in your class?
- How would you handle cheating?
- How would you handle a student who refused to do what you asked?
- Should schools practice corporal punishment? Why or why not?
- If students tell you they have engaged in some illegal or immoral activity, what would you do?

Professional Activities and Knowledge

- What do you think about the current events or happenings in education? What is the most exciting event happening in the area of education today?
- In what professional organizations do you hold memberships?
- How have you recently improved your professional skills? What are your plans for future improvement of professional skills?
- Comment on some leaders in education. Cite several authorities in your subject of preparation and comment on them.
- What professional journals do you read regularly? What have you read in the last six months or year?
- Do you plan to continue your education?

At the end of the interview, some employers give the applicant a chance to "sell themselves" by answering one of their own questions.

Examples

Interviewer: "What questions have I not asked, that you wish I would have raised?"

Interviewer: "What were you prepared to tell me that I have not asked? And, why is this particular information important to communicate?"

Questions for the Employer

As covered earlier, well-thought-out questions are an important part of the interview. Effective questions are:

1. Tailored to the particular position and district.
2. Used to gather information and locate needs, so you can bring out information on how you could fill those needs.
3. Used to confirm facts, showing you have done your homework and have thought about how you might make a contribution.

Selectively choose questions. An interviewer's time is limited.

It is difficult to make a list of questions for the employer, because each interview, employer, position, district, and community is unique. An appropriate question in one situation would be inappropriate in another. The following is a very general list of possibilities you may consider adapting to your situation:

- What are your current employment opportunities or anticipated opportunities?
- Why is this position open?
- What do you consider ideal experience or education for this position?
- Do you use ability grouping in your schools?
- Would I be part of a team teaching situation? Open classrooms?
- Could you tell me about the other educators who would be working with me?
- Are extracurricular assignments available for teachers interested and qualified?
- Does your district offer faculty in-service training days during the school year?
- What reading series (or math series) is currently being used?
- Do you have an active parent-teacher organization?
- What percentage of your graduates continue their education?
- What is the retention rate for secondary students?
- What types of support personnel are employed by this district (counselors, coordinators, language and reading specialists)?
- Are computers available for classroom use?
- Do you have a media center, learning center, resource materials?
- What is the largest single problem facing your staff now?
- Will I be expected to maintain office hours in addition to teaching?

Interview Follow-Up

There are important steps to follow after the interview. Begin with a written self-evaluation. Review and analyze your presentation. Ask yourself:

- What do I know about this position and district that I did not know before?
- How would I answer those same interview questions next time?
- How could I have improved the interview?
- If offered a position there, would I accept?
- How do I feel about this position, district, employer?
- What did I learn about myself?

As soon as possible, write your reactions to these questions. Also, record as many questions asked as you remember. Not only does this process help put the meeting in proper perspective, but the information can be beneficial when preparing for your next interview. (Self-analysis makes every interview a learning experience.) In your record keeping system, include these personal notes with interview facts—when the interview was held, with whom (name and title), and the address and phone number of the school district represented. (See the section in chapter 3, "Keep Accurate Records.")

Another after-interview step is to provide the district with any needed documents to complete the application process. Promptly follow directions or special instructions given during the interview, such as visiting a school or meeting with a department head.

Always write a thank-you letter for the employer's time and consideration. Do this no matter how the interview went. There are several reasons for this formality. It is a gesture of courtesy. It emphasizes your image as a true professional. It brings the employer's attention back to you and the interview. And it gives you a chance to further emphasize some strong selling point you may have forgotten to mention or thought of later.

Do not exceed one page. Stick to the point. Send one personal note of thanks to the screening committee, or you may choose to thank each committee member individually.

Be patient in hearing from a district or school. For various reasons it may take a long period of time to contact you. A question at the end of the interview, "When can I expect to hear from you?" may give insight into the length of time to expect.

On page 145 is an example of a thank-you letter following an interview. It is based on the resume by Chris A. Compton, a high school instructor desiring a career move from Washington to Montana. After an interview with the personnel director, Chris was instructed to meet with the high school principal and staff. They also received a letter of appreciation.

CONTRACTS AND PROFESSIONAL ETHICS

A contract is a legal document which clarifies the terms of an agreement between two parties. It is designed for the mutual protection of both the educator and the board of education. It may include extracurricular activities as well as classroom responsibilities. Most districts have a master contract that specifies exact number of working days, evaluation procedures, salary schedule, insurance and retirement plans, and guidelines for leaves and termi-

Sample Interview Follow-Up Letter

April 10, 1989

1001 Arlington Lane
Meadville, Washington 90000

Carol M. Clevor
Personnel Director, Secondary Education
Grand School District
777 Campbell Avenue
Stevenson, Montana 66666

Dear Ms. Clevor:

Thank you for the time you gave me this morning. The position of Senior High History Instructor at Fredonia High School is of great interest to me. After talking with you, and after visiting with Mr. Calvin and the faculty, I am very enthusiastic about the prospect of joining their staff. The overall positive climate and dedication to the academic progress and self-esteem of each student is apparent.

One point not brought out in our interview which may be of interest to you is I have currently completed a workshop focused on preparing students for university entrance exams. Mr. Calvin mentioned the need for such information. I would welcome the opportunity to work with the other staff members in developing a study program for seniors.

With my experience, accomplishments, and passion for educating, I feel confident I can contribute to the development of the history curriculum and positive learning activities of Grand School District. As requested, I have arranged to have an official transcript sent to you. It was indeed a pleasure to meet you and the superior staff of Fredonia High.

Sincerely,

Chris A. Compton

---

nation of employment. An individual contract may state that all terms included in the master contract are part of the agreement.

Seldom are contracts offered at the conclusion of an interview. Interviewers need time to consider all candidates. This is to your advantage, as you also need time to reflect on the position and district in order to make a sound decision.

The interval between the interview and the offer of a contract depends on many variables. References are checked. Each candidate's "fitness" for the position is evaluated. The employer may have consultations with screening committee members. Finally, district needs enter into the decision. Growth patterns, transfers, reassignments, sabbaticals, maternity leaves, specific staff needs, and possible regrouping of existing faculties are all influencing factors.

During the waiting time, serious candidates persist in job search techniques and proceed with further interviewing. They also continue to gather new information and reassess and evaluate their needs.

Contracts may be offered by telephone, in person, sent by cable, or mailed. When a contract is presented, you have a time frame in which to accept or reject it. However you decide, it is important to respond promptly. In deciding to accept, return the signed contract with a brief cover letter confirming your acceptance. In doing so, also contact other schools where you applied and inform them you have accepted a contract. This is the one time it is perfectly acceptable to use a form (see Sample Form Letter).

Everyone appreciates this courtesy. The district can remove your application from their files, eliminating wasted time, money, and energy trying to contact you. (Also send one to your college placement center.)

If deciding to reject the offer, send a letter expressing your appreciation and state that you are not accepting the offer. Once the employers have presented a contract, they are on hold until informed of your decision. They cannot offer that position to anyone else until you respond. As an act of courtesy and professionalism, inform them of your decision as soon as possible.

FACT: A contract is a legally binding document. Once you place your signature on it, you are lawfully and ethically committed to fulfill the contract obligations. You are no longer free to pursue any other options. (By the way, a verbal agreement may be equally binding.)

Do not make the mistake of signing two contracts. The employer may take legal action against you, even resulting in having your teaching certificate revoked. Once you have signed an agreement, live with it and do not look back. The significance of doing your homework, both in internal self-assessment and external information gathering, is particularly evident at this crucial decision-making period.

There are exceptional circumstances in which you can ask to be released from a contract. For example, your spouse is unexpectedly transferred to another location, serious family or health problems arise, personal problems occur, or a career change becomes available (such as the chance to move into administration). When your reason is legitimate and you handle the situation in a professional manner, most employers make every effort to accommodate your request. Keep in mind that much time and effort enters into the hiring

Sample Form Letter

Inside Address
Date

Dear _____ :

    Please be advised by this form letter that I have an application on file with your school district. As of this date, I have accepted a position at _____ and am no longer available for employment. Please remove my application from your current active files.

    Thank you for your consideration.

Sincerely,

---

process. Choosing to release you depends upon the availability of finding a suitable replacement in the allotted time.

YOUR PROFESSIONAL IMAGE

From writing your first business letter to signing the contract, always conduct business within a highly professional framework. A professional is one who does things in a professional manner. Professionals

- write business letters.
- do their homework.
- start early on their job search campaign.
- accurately type application forms.
- keep records.
- follow up on all correspondence.
- keep their placement file and documents up to date.
- submit professional resumes.
- comply promptly and accurately with the hiring procedures of each employer.
- provide accurate and current information on all records and forms.
- join professional associations.
- budget money for expenses.
- are professional in dress and manner.

- are punctual for all appointments.
- answer interview questions with honesty and integrity.
- notify school districts where they applied and their college career office when they accept a position.
- answer all communications from employers immediately and in a businesslike manner.
- sign only one contract.
- honor contracts (both verbal and written).
- fulfill professional responsibilities with integrity.
- are ethical and responsible in all actions.

WHO IS CHOSEN?

During the final interviewing stage, those still in the game are all qualified, capable, and knowledgeable candidates. The question is, "Who is the best fit?" Which one of these qualified applicants best meets the needs of the school, the district, and the community? The professional selected is liked by the interviewer(s) and has convinced the employer that he/she is the best candidate to get the job done. The employer feels this candidate

- is enthusiastic about the position.
- is self-confident.
- looks appropriate.
- is reliable.
- contributes beyond the regular duties.
- is a strong team player.
- helps solve problems and meets needs.
- "fits" with the established faculty.
- matches the district, the established faculty, and the community in philosophies, values, and beliefs.

WHAT IF I AM NOT HIRED?

Rejection is part of the job hunt process. Although it is painful, it is also a part of life. For every position available, one applicant is hired. Out of the 100 applicants for a position, ninety-nine are rejected. Yet all 100 had the confidence to take the necessary risk in order to succeed.

Although we can vividly recall our own failures, we tend to watch and hear only of the success of others. Everyone who has ever tried has at some time failed. Rejection cannot stop you unless you let it.

When you do not get the position you want, do not return to your old job at the local amusement park. Stay involved in the field of education. Getting your foot in the door continues to be a truly good approach for future employment. Substitute, aide, tutor, or take a part-time or temporary teaching position. Make contacts, network, join and get involved in a professional association. Keep in contact with your college career center and districts of interest. Also, find out how long districts keep applications on file. Usually, one must re-submit an application after one year. (This is good, as yours will need to be up dated.)

You may not get the position you want the first time around. Put forth full effort to make it happen the next time around. The odds are certainly against you unless you remain positive and confident.

Rejections result in feelings of insecurity and uncertainty. Yet, not getting the position you desire may have nothing to do with you as a person. ("Was it something I did? something I said?") Remember, various factors influence the final hiring decisions—grade level or subject requirements, needs for special abilities or characteristics, sudden changes in faculty requirements, budget and curriculum considerations, decreasing enrollment, stiff competition, or large numbers of qualified candidates with few openings.

Use setbacks as an opportunity to gain self-knowledge, re-evaluate your priorities and values, and examine your original goals:

- Are you willing to travel further or move?
- Are you realistic and flexible concerning grade level or subject preferences?
- What insights did you gain from your actions?
- Did you do the right things at the right time?
- How will you approach your goals the second time around?
- What can you do now to accelerate your progress?
- How can you increase career competencies and/or salesmanship of your qualities?

Handle rejection intelligently. Use it as a chance for personal growth. Keep a sense of perspective and an awareness of alternatives. Continue to gather information and gain knowledge. With new experience, up date your placement/credentials file and highlight current qualifications on your resumes, cover letters, and application forms.

Getting what you want depends on your willingness to persist and steadily progress toward the realization of your goal. These efforts are truly a worthwhile investment, for there are few things in life more important or gratifying than finding your right career fit.

FINAL THOUGHTS

The first task in your career search is to know *what you want to do* and *where you want to be* in the professional educator's world. Find your niche through ongoing personal self-assessment and information gathering. Prepare thoroughly and meticulously to get the position that is your best possible professional match. Implement your plan of action with energy and perseverance. Continually accumulate information, make it a learning process, enjoy the search, and keep a clear vision of your goal. The right position will not find you—you must find it. When you do, work hard, get involved, be honest with yourself and with others, foster new ideas, build on your strengths, combine natural talent with dedicated hard work, and be productive and resourceful. There is no greater feeling than giving your best in a career you love.

Nowhere do we say any of this is easy. There is no easy way. The future is a constant challenge. An old Indian saying confirms, "The gates of excellence are surrounded by a sea of sweat."

CHA5TER

Positions in Educational Administration

T here are a multitude of administrative levels, departments, and divisions in the educational career field. Each district within each state has full control over developing and governing its own administrative organizational structure. No two districts have the (exact) same management system, and there is no one standard procedure for administrative hiring. There is, however, basic information, essential knowledge, and necessary skills that all applicants need for a successful entry into this marketplace.

Although the job market for administrators is beginning to improve (predictions say 40 percent of current administrators will retire within ten years), obtaining your desired position may not be easy. The attainment of your career goal depends on your efforts, perseverance, preparation, and the successful completion of all necessary tasks.

To maximize your chances of achieving your career goal, you, as a job candidate, need solid understanding of the groundwork presented in chapters 1-4. These chapters have provided the nuts and bolts of your job search by explaining the steps involved in the hiring process, the necessity of developing convincing and effective marketing tools, the importance of having an organized plan of action, and vital information for increasing your chances of success in the interview.

The following section builds on this information, highlighting the important principles, knowledge, guidelines, and strategies that are unique to those seeking positions in administration.

INFORMATION TO KNOW

Self-Assessment and Knowledge of the Position

Self-assessment is the important first step when entering the job market. Who am I? What do I want? What do I have to offer? And how am I a unique, special human being?

These questions require considerable thought during this transitional period. (See the section in chapter 1 on self-assessment.)

A process of continuous self-assessment is enhanced with knowledge of the position and the employer. This combined information integrates you with your career search, forming a powerful combination. A thorough process of self-assessment and information gathering provides:

- career direction by determining and defining your professional and personal objectives.
- valuable material for developing effective sales brochures and preparing for interviews. (Self-knowledge, combined with insight of employer needs, determines which attributes and experiences to highlight to best sell yourself for the desired position.)
- self-confidence, leading the way to intelligent decision making.

During the process of self-assessment and information gathering, applicants for positions in administration need to place special emphasis on the following three areas:

1. How and where you fit in your professional world.
2. Where you see yourself going in your profession.
3. The unique qualities you bring to this position.

How and Where Do You Fit in Your Professional World?

Do you have the required education, preparation, credentials, abilities, knowledge, and professional experience to be a qualified, competitive candidate for this career move? To answer this question, an applicant needs the following:

- a thorough understanding of the qualifications of the position.
- to study the career paths of other administrators in the area.
- to gather all information possible concerning this unique position, district, and community.

Understand the Qualifications.   Begin by obtaining a printed job description. Usually the major qualifications and the desired qualifications are described. Positions in administration depend a great deal on a candidate's past and present academic and professional accomplishments, plus the ability to sell the candidate's unique value to the employer. Therefore, a thorough analysis of your background, in relation to the employer's needs and wants, is an essential element.

An important question for administrative applicants is, "Have I made a logical career progression toward this professional objective?" Usually, administrators move slowly and methodically toward their ultimate career goal. It is highly unlikely that an instructor from a small rural town with three years experience would attain a position as principal of an inner city school of 1800 students (no matter how much one desires the move or feels competent in handling the job). Most people are not capable of making giant leaps in job responsibility, and most employers would not take a chance on hiring someone who is not professionally prepared. We are not saying administrative candidates are restricted to only small, modest steps in the progression of their career achievements. However, we are saying planned, systematic, and orderly career moves are the path to success in administration.

Indiscriminately applying for any and all openings is not smart. Random application for positions that are not an appropriate match for you wastes valuable time and effort (yours and the employer's). It demonstrates to the district that you do not have a realistic view of your own qualifications. The employer also feels you do not fully comprehend the responsibilities of the position, or have an understanding of the many qualified applicants who can present stronger backgrounds.

Study Career Paths.   Examine the career and academic paths of administrators in your geographical area of interest (especially new administrators). While you are not confined to follow in their (exact) footsteps, backgrounds of past and present administrators are an indication of current and future hiring guidelines. Discover the academic and professional steps and stages they executed to reach their current assignments. What events, education, and training pointed them to where they are now?

Districts and employers vary greatly. An applicant may be well suited and qualified in one area, but not in another. Know the qualifications in the area in which you are applying. Ask yourself, "To be a qualified candidate for the position of my choice, what kinds of experience, education, and knowledge do I need to best prepare me for reaching my professional goal? What can I do now to begin preparing for and moving toward this career objective?" (See the section "Professional Preparation Required" later in this chapter.)

If you come to the conclusion that you are a qualified candidate, ask yourself, "Based on self-understanding, other administrators' career paths, and this unique position—what experiences, preparation, accomplishments, knowledge, and abilities do I highlight (in my paperwork and in the interview) to best sell me for this career move?" (What part of your past best markets you for this desired future?)

In itself, being an exceptionally qualified candidate does not get you the job. Applicants must convince the district of their worth. The more you know about the position and how it matches you, the qualifications and preparation required, the needs and wants of the employer, their specific problems and how you can help solve them, the more effective salesperson you can be.

Gather Information. Do your wants, values, interests, career and life goals, and basic philosophy match the position and the community? To answer this question and also to market yourself as a knowledgeable candidate, you must gather information on all aspects of this position and community.

Visit schools and districts. Study the area, physical conditions of the buildings, the community, housing, recreation, and all other aspects of interest. Call ahead for a structured visit of the district office or of individual schools. Read district literature, the school and community newspaper, visit the Chamber of Commerce, and talk to people in the district.

Chapter 3 examines the important "Information to Know" before application. Adapt the questions presented in that section to your situation, then place emphasis on the following questions, which are specifically designed for administrative candidates:

- What is this position and why is it open? Is it a new position or a current vacancy? If a vacancy, why did the previous administrator leave?
- What kind of a position is it? Will you be part of a team? If so, who are the other members of the team? Is it a strong management team?
- What is the morale and reputation of the faculty(s) and administration?
- If a superintendent position, who are the board members? Do you feel you can work comfortably with their basic philosophy?
- What are the goals of the district? What are their major concerns? Do you feel you will be able to work together effectively to reach those goals and solve problems? How do you feel the goals can best be realized?
- What problems do you anticipate? What experiences/preparation do you bring to help you with these new responsibilities?

Understanding the qualifications required, knowledge of the career paths of administrators in your desired area, and gathering information on the unique position, helps determine how and where you fit in your professional world.

Where Do You See Yourself Going in Your Profession?

Where you see yourself (in your professional life and personal life) in the next five, ten, or fifteen years is another crucial area of knowledge for administrative candidates.

Of course, achieving a present goal is necessary before consideration of a subsequent move. However, visualizing and projecting into the possibilities of your professional future is an important task. The more you know about yourself—what you want now and later—the better you know in which direction to aim your sights in order to reach your objectives. The decisions you make today determine your future.

A question often asked is, "How long should I stay in one position?" There is no absolute answer; however, three years is generally accepted as a minimum. Moving every year can get you a reputation as a job hopper, whereas staying too long in one place can indicate a lack of initiative or drive.

The type of move is important. Was each one an advance, a promotion? Did you have a series of in-district moves or between-district moves? The quality of work completed is equally important. Programs developed, new skills acquired, projects completed, and positive working relationships established determine how quickly you move on. Gaining valuable skills, experiences, and accomplishments sell you for future positions. The following questions are for guidance in determining where you see yourself going:

- In general, what are your overall professional and personal objectives? What position now will help you attain future goals?
- Where do you see yourself in five years? ten years? fifteen years?
- How far do you hope to move along the administrative ladder? What is the next step in your career progression?
- Are you willing to move (geographically) to get what you want? (Increasing your boundaries strengthens your chances of attaining your goals.)

The following questions are for guidance in determining where you see yourself going when evaluating a particular opening:

- Will this be a positive career move for you? Is it a move up? How will this position help you grow professionally? Will this position lead to future professional goals?
- What does this area offer for future educational goals? Recreational? Cultural? Religious? Personal?

- What new experiences and knowledge do you hope to gain from this experience? Will you be challenged and motivated in this position?
- What are you leaving behind in accepting this position? Why do you desire this career change? Is it the right professional move at the right time?
- Is this a growing geographical area? If not, what does this mean for your future as an administrator?
- Will this be a positive move for you and your family? What are the living conditions in this area? Expenses? Will you (and your family) be happy here? Does your philosophy of living match the community? What will be your "visibility" in the community? And your family's? (Small community? Urban? Rural?)
- Does the salary and benefit package match your personal needs?

What Are the Unique Qualities You Bring to a Position?

One of the most important reasons for undergoing a thorough self-assessment is to fully appreciate and understand the unique qualities you bring to a position. Remember, the first step to good salesmanship is knowing the product. Only then can you effectively market your unique qualities. After completing the self-assessment questionnaire in chapter 1, continue with the following questions:

- How are you a special candidate? What makes you stand out from the others?
- How will you make a difference? How will your qualifications and abilities meet the employer's needs? How will you make a contribution?
- Do you fit this position and does this position fit you? How do you know you fit? What strengths (education, experience, preparation, abilities, knowledge, qualifications, skills) do you bring to this position? Does this position take advantage of your strengths?
- Do you feel qualified to handle the problems? What weaknesses must you overcome to solve these problems?

Smart applicants for positions in administration do not underestimate the importance of a continuous process of self-assessment and information gathering. Understanding how and where you fit, where you are going, and the unique qualities you bring to your profession are the beginning steps in finding your "right fit" in administration.

REQUIRED PROFESSIONAL PREPARATION

At one time, a popular football or basketball coach or well-liked educator with administrative certification was typically picked as the next administrator. This was part of the "good ol' boy" system.

Times have changed. Equal opportunity and affirmative action, large numbers of qualified candidates, and greater emphasis on the importance of knowledgeable educational leadership have greatly impacted the administrative marketplace. Today, obtaining administrative certification gives you the opportunity to be employable as an administrator. Convincing the schoolboard or selection committee that you are their "right fit" is another matter.

There is a continuous nationwide effort toward significant changes in the preparation and continuing development of educational leaders. Increasingly, those who are successful in the administrative marketplace have expanded time and effort to become professionally prepared. The professional development required of administrators can be outlined in the following four steps:

1. Gain additional academic preparation.
2. Become an active, involved member in a professional organization(s).
3. Pursue professional development workshops/programs.
4. Become actively involved in school district leadership activities.

More frequently, a doctorate degree, a second masters degree, or a specialist degree is a prerequisite to success in the administrative marketplace. This holds true whether aspiring toward your first administrative position or attempting to move up the professional ladder (assistant principal to principal, assistant superintendent to superintendent, or any other district level administrative position). Failure to become academically qualified puts the candidate at a tremendous disadvantage with competition.

In addition, membership and active involvement in professional associations are extremely important for career advancement in administration. To be considered as an upcoming educational leader, one must be recognized by others and be associated with those who are educational leaders. Membership in professional associations allows you to gain information, insight, service, leadership, and provides valuable networking opportunities. (See the section in chapter 2 on professional associations.)

Employers seek professionals who are involved in their profession. Join the American Association of School Administrators and your own state's association of school administrators. You can enter as either a regular or associate (beginner) member. State associations usually have a number of subdivisions (superintendent, secondary, middle school, elementary, educational services, and possibly a higher education division). There is an area of interest for everyone seeking a career in administration.

Within the divisions, there are frequently numerous committees offering opportunities for service and recognition. These range from membership and program committees to groups addressing the professional development of administrators to special committees (such as meeting the needs of small and rural schools).

Most state school administrator associations also offer members a number of professional development opportunities. Frequently, these are in the form of programs, workshops, or institutes that may be a day or more in length. They are taught or sponsored by members of the association who are educational leaders of the state. The following topics are a sample of such professional development activities:

Leadership Training
Experienced Administrator Management Programs
Aspiring Administrator Management Training
Qualified Evaluators Institute
Hiring and Firing Workshops
Negotiations Institute

Many state associations, in cooperation with school districts, school board associations, and universities, also sponsor Administrator Assessment Centers or Academies. These centers or academies offer training, professional development, and evaluation (or grading) for administrators. (In an assessment center, potential administrators perform simulated activities and are graded and given feedback on essential management skills.) These centers are becoming increasingly popular and are a vital part of professional development for administrators.

School districts offer numerous and varied opportunities for professional development and leadership roles. All districts provide various volunteer activities, such as participating as a member of in-district committees. These committees deal with a wide range of topics from curriculum revision, to career ladders, to parent and community involvement. Many large districts have their own administrator training programs.

The opportunities to gain experience and become involved and recognized in leadership roles are readily available to those who aspire to become administrators or to advance within the ranks. Following the right steps in professional development is an important key to your future success in the administrative marketplace.

PREPARING THE PAPERWORK

Your Sales Brochures

Effective, convincing sales brochures are your tickets into the job market. The resume, cover letter, application form, and placement file are thoroughly reviewed in chapter 2. This section points out special considerations for candidates seeking administrative positions.

Documents submitted by applicants for positions in administration must clearly emphasize the following three areas:

1. Demonstrate an understanding of the position, the responsibilities, and the duties required.
2. Based on your background (accomplishments, knowledge, preparation, education, experience), show how you qualify to fulfill the responsibilities and demonstrate how you will make a dynamic contribution.
3. Clearly communicate how you "fit" the position, the district, and the community.

As emphasized in chapter 2, there is no such thing as an all purpose resume. An effective sales brochure is designed to fit the position by focusing attention on the applicant's qualifications and attributes that match the employer's needs.

A common resume mistake administrative candidates often make is stating responsibilities of their current assignment, yet do nothing to prove how they qualify for the desired position. Highlight professional experiences, preparation, accomplishments, and academic achievements in light of how your background has prepared you for this new transition. In other words, tailor your paperwork to sell your potential. Use action statements and accomplishment oriented results. (See the section in chapter 2, "Using Action Words.")

The following are two descriptions of professional experience written by an assistant principal applying for a position as principal. The first simply describes the responsibilities of the current job. The second example highlights specific accomplishments, includes results that sell potential, and creates a professional image through the use of category titles.

Example 1

PROFESSIONAL EXPERIENCE: Assistant Principal, Glendale School District, Colton City, Mayberry Middle School, 1985-1988. 300 students, grades 6-8. 20 staff.

Responsible for discipline, attendance, and extracurricular activities. Duties included developing and evaluating the special education program, and leading parent advisory group. Observed and evaluated teachers.

Example 2

PROFESSIONAL EXPERIENCE: Assistant Principal, Glendale School District, Colton City, Mayberry Middle School, 1985-1988. 300 students, grades 6-8. 20 staff.

NEW PROGRAMS: Played key role in development and evaluation of Special Education Program—concepts to be incorporated into two other schools. Student discipline and attendance problems decreased 40 percent with introduction of student-management approach.

EFFECTIVE LEADERSHIP: Parent's Advisory Group Leader—concern for improved math program led to series of discussion groups between instructors and parents. Positive results: goals and comprehensive math plan specified, parent volunteer program incorporated, increased communication and rapport. (Incorporated management ideas from Administrator's Assessment Center, 1988.)

PRODUCTIVE EVALUATIONS: End of year Teacher Evaluations —staff input helped determine evaluation criteria and assessment procedure. Group involvement and team decision making brought about notable boost of staff morale.

Include professional growth activities in your resume. As mentioned before, membership and active participation in professional affiliations are a key ingredient in opening the door for careers in administration. These associations are an important component toward development of professional competencies and provide a major networking resource during your job search. Therefore, professional growth and association involvement is obviously a significant category of your resume. Here are examples to include in this area:

Current association memberships and affiliations
Offices held
Workshops, conferences, conventions, and programs attended
Leadership activities
Academies of learning and assessment centers participation

Committee participation and leadership
Professional service and volunteer activities

Publications and presentations are additional professional growth selling points in your document. Publications include a thesis or dissertation, curriculum materials, special projects, district guidelines, articles, pamphlets, and books. State the title, name of the publication, and date. For curriculum guidelines and materials, report the grade level and subject. Presentations include speeches, participation on panels, slide or tape shows, radio or TV talks, and community and association presentations. State the title, the group or organization involved, and the date.

References are located in your placement/credentials file. Applicants for educational administration can include additional references on their resume. These can be listed under the category, "Additional References Not in Placement File." Give the name, title, address and telephone number. Be very selective in choosing references. Always ask permission to use a person's name as a reference, make sure they support your professional objective, and inform them of your career goals.

The sample resume on the following pages describes an assistant principal from Nebraska who is applying for a position as a junior high or middle school principal in California. Remember, each resume must also include a personalized cover letter. (See the section in chapter 2 on cover letters.)

Additional Materials

Administrative candidates may wish to send additional materials to the screening committee to support their candidacy. (Always check with the school board or search committee to inquire if additional materials will be accepted.)

This can be an effective sales approach, if materials are carefully selected. (Do not send originals.) Every proposal, curriculum guide, report, or other supplementary document must clearly support your career objective. It does not help your candidacy (and it could hurt) to send an abundance of any and all materials. You could also bring selected materials with you to the interview to strengthen your salesmanship.

Keep accurate records and copies of all materials submitted. A method for creating a plan of action and following through on all activities is fully covered in chapter 3.

Terry L. Wasserman

2345 Hamilton Lane   Chapman City, Nebraska 55666   (400) 123-6543

PROFESSIONAL OBJECTIVE

Desire position as a Junior High or Middle School Principal where there is a need for maintaining excellent staff and student morale, strong communication skills, and development of new goals and programs to meet curriculum and discipline needs.

QUALIFICATIONS

Effective leadership...dynamic human relations skills...new program development...confident and creative management style...active community member...student management programs...innovative ideas...parent participation

CREDENTIALS

Secondary Principal Certification, California, pending.
Secondary Principal Certification, Nebraska, 1986.
Secondary Teaching Certification, Nebraska, 1982.

PROFESSIONAL EXPERIENCE

Assistant Principal—Oxnard Middle School, Northeast School District, 500 student population, Grades 6-9, 25 staff. Oxnard, Nebraska, 1987-present.

Supervision and Public Relations: Organized and directed extra- curricular activities for extended day needs. Music and drama workshops huge success! Created new system of student management, significantly improving discipline and attendance. Supervised gifted, bilingual, and special education programs. Established parent help groups, increasing participation 35 percent in the second year.

Administration and Evaluation: Played key role in selection of teachers. Co-authored new staff evaluation system—superintendent plans to introduce procedure to other principals. Evaluated programs, textbooks, curriculum, budget, and school maintenance. Welcomed input from staff and parents. Curriculum development committee leader—evaluation and selection of 7th-8th grade English objectives and supplementary materials, 1988. Presented results to three schools.

Educator—Bakerman Middle School, Northeast School District, English and history, 7th and 8th grade, 1982-1987. Successfully organized team teaching approach for English classes. Served on 7th grade English and history curriculum development committee, 1985-87. Faculty advisor for student government, 1986-87. Presented workshop to English department based on materials from the National Education Association Convention, "New Trends in Teaching Writing," 1986.

ACADEMIC PREPARATION

Master of Arts Degree—School Administration, Western University, 1986.
    Coldwell Scholarship Award.

Bachelor of Arts—English major, history minor, Western University, 1982.
    College newspaper, two years. Dean's honor list, 1980-1982.

Sample Resume *(continued)*

PROFESSIONAL TRAINING

Graduate of Nebraska School Administrator's "Principal's Assessment Center," 1986.

PROFESSIONAL AFFILIATIONS AND ACTIVITIES

National Association of Secondary School Principals, 1985-present.
National Education Association, 1982-present.
Nebraska School Administrators, 1985-present, secretary 1986.
American Association of School Administrators, 1985-present.
American Association of School Administrators, National Convention, New York, 1988.
Nebraska School Administrators, State Convention, 1986.
     Served on panel discussion, "Current Trends in Middle Schools."
     Conference: "So You Want To Be An Administrator."
National Education Association, 1987 Convention
     Presented speech, "Our Middle Schools in Transition."

COMMUNITY AND CIVIC ACTIVITIES

Chamber of Commerce, 1985-present.
Kiwanis International, 1982-present. Social Chairman, 1984.

UP-TO-DATE PLACEMENT/CREDENTIALS FILE

Career and Placement Office, Northwest University,
     344 West Mayfair Drive, Dalton, Nebraska, 98765 (700) 999-6666. File No. 3876.

ADDITIONAL REFERENCES NOT IN PLACEMENT FILE

Dr. James L. Parker, Professor, Western University
     1232 Stanford Way, University City, Nebraska 99880 (655) 765-9800

Robert M. Abbot, President, Nebraska School Administrators Association
     6654 Newell Lane, Marymont, Nebraska 97766 (877) 655-0099

PERSONAL VISION

Believe schools today can reach objectives under the influence of strong, shared leadership. My job: provide the structural support, effective leadership, open communication, guidance, and motivation to encourage putting innovative ideas into everyday practice.

Placement/Credentials File and Letters of Reference

Your placement (or credentials) file and letters of reference are an integral part of application. See chapter 2 for a full description of this category. A word of warning for candidates who attended several colleges while completing degree and credential programs: Consolidate all materials into one college file. *Never send partial files from several institutions.*

A marketable placement file includes up-to-date information and contains three to six carefully selected letters of reference. (An experienced administrator could possibly have a maximum of ten.) Begin with your current supervisors and/or the superintendent. Other possibilities include board members, university faculty, members of professional associations, academy instructors, and local business people. Effective letters document teaching and administration experiences, extracurricular responsibilities, and achievements and accomplishments which point you in the direction of your professional objective.

Keep your placement file current. Outdated and incomplete information hurts your chances of employment. As you complete studies and degrees, gain new experiences and preparation, serve internships, volunteer for special projects, serve on committees, or learn new skills, document your file with current statements of accomplishments. This new information should also be incorporated into your resumes and in current letters of reference.

In the past few years, employers have been asking for additional references in order to get an overall picture of the candidate. You may be asked to submit a letter from a peer, from someone who reports to you, a community member, a teacher, a counselor, a member of a parent support group, or a student. The district hopes to gain understanding of your management style, your leadership capabilities, your communication and human relationship skills, and your ability to work with all types of people. These are in addition to the references listed in your placement file. As with all references, choose people who like you and your work, understand and support your objective, and write well.

LOCATING OPENINGS

Candidates seeking employment opportunities in administration need to place special emphasis on networking. *Contacts continue to be a main source of job information.* Important contacts develop and grow with participation in professional associations and activities, and with community involvement. Employers hire people they know or know about. Join national and state professional associations in your field of interest. Become active, attend meetings, get involved on committees and special projects, and get to know others. Also become involved in selected community activities.

Job opportunity information is often located in professional association literature and newsletters. College placement/career centers contain notebooks, bulletins, journals, and vacancy lists. *Education Week* and other journals related to your career field contain job opportunity information, as do school board associations in various states. (See chapter 3 for a full description of sources of openings in the educational marketplace.)

UNDERSTANDING THE HIRING PROCESS

Understanding the hiring process is an important element when entering the marketplace. There are, of course, major differences between the hiring process of an assistant principal in a small elementary school and the process involved in hiring a superintendent for a large metropolitan school district. In addition, the screening and selection process for each position varies greatly from district to district, region to region, and state to state. It is important to remind administrative candidates that each district is responsible for developing and supervising its own administrative recruiting, screening, and hiring processes.

Because the various districts operate independently, there are numerous and diverse employment methods and procedures used. Part of understanding the hiring process for administrators comes from doing your homework.

Find out how the hiring process is carried out in your area for the position you seek. There are many variables from initial paper screening, to in-house screening committees, to assorted varieties and numbers of interviews, to diverse selection criteria, to negotiating your salary and contract.

Seek advice and guidance from people holding positions that are of interest to you. Within your current district or in a district of interest, talk to administrators currently hired or ones who applied for positions. Find out what worked and what did not work, and gather information on the screening and interviewing procedures. You also gain information through association meetings and contacts. Many times workshops are offered to help new or current administrators understand the hiring process.

A way for a beginner to start gathering information is by asking your principal or superintendent to let you participate in the selection process for a position in administration. Read all paperwork submitted by candidates. Notice the ones selected for interviews based on their sales brochures. Critically observe all selection and hiring procedures. Although each employer is different, you gain valuable knowledge and insight in this experience.

Although there are as many different hiring procedures as there are districts, some often-used styles can be found. In all but the superintendency, one common method of selecting administrators is by district-appointed in-house screening (or selection) committees. These committees consist of teachers and administrators, sometimes school board members, parents, or even students. They decide on the methods and techniques to be used in the initial paper screening, questions to be asked in the interview, and selection criteria.

Frequently there is an initial screening interview, followed by a second in-depth interview. Applicants may be invited for a group interview, proceed through a series of meetings with individuals, or have any combination of encounters. Candidates may be asked to view films and write teaching evaluations. Sometimes they are asked to submit written answers to specific questions. However the screening is accomplished, all districts place a high value on excellence in oral and written communication.

The decision for a position as superintendent is made by the school board members. This process is accomplished by using their own hiring system, having the departing superintendent aid their selection, employing the services of a consulting service, or creating a panel of advisors from universities or a non-educational consulting group.

It is the school board's decision to determine how the application and screening process will function, and the final selection for the position of superintendent is in their hands.

Doing your homework is the key to obtaining current and accurate hiring information. Find out how it's done for the position you desire, in your district of interest.

THE INTERVIEW

The critical task of interviewing is fully covered in chapter 4. Review the concepts and adapt the commonly asked interview questions to your situation. As with screening and selection of finalists, interviewing processes vary greatly between states, regions, and districts. Wherever you are interviewed, all administrative candidates should be prepared to answer questions regarding these concepts:

- management style
- methods of fulfilling duties
- curriculum considerations
- finance and budgeting philosophy
- working relationships—with supervisors, staff, parents, students
- community involvement

- staff evaluation and hiring procedures
- negotiations

The following sample interview questions are designed for administrative candidates:

- What are your life goals and how does this position fit your plan? Why do you want to make a job change at this time?
- How would you successfully bring about a needed change in your school? Or in a program? Give an example of a change you successfully implemented.
- How would you encourage involvement of students in school activities? How would you encourage involvement of parents in school activities?
- What is the biggest problem you have had as an administrator? How did you handle it? What project was your greatest success as an administrator?
- How would you describe your management style? How do you inspire team work?
- Describe a project you developed and carried through to the end. How did it benefit the school/district?
- What experiences have you had with goal setting?
- What are the three most important duties of this position? How are you qualified to fulfill those duties?
- How would you encourage interdepartmental communication?
- What actions would you take to improve morale of a faculty?
- What is the role of counseling and guidance in the schools? Do you feel career guidance is important? Describe a program for career guidance that you would like to have in your school.
- What problem-solving techniques have you used successfully? Give an example of a problem solved using this technique.
- Tell us your organization method for faculty and staff meetings.
- What is your experience with scheduling classes?
- How would you handle severe discipline problems? What discipline programs have you used with success? What is your opinion in regard to due process rights for students and parents in discipline matters?
- What are the key elements in maintaining good discipline in a school? What is the principal's role in maintaining discipline? How do you feel about suspension? Expulsion? Corporal punishment? Dismissal? In-school suspension?

- How have you been involved in student activity funds or budgets? What is your philosophy for developing a budget? What steps would you take to reduce a budget?
- How do you feel about negotiations and collective bargaining?
- How would you formulate policies in budgeting, personnel, curriculum, discipline, public relations?
- How do you feel about "extras" in schools—the importance of athletics, art, music...?
- What curriculum changes do you see ahead? What are the current trends in education? How do you see public support for schools in the future?
- What can we do to ensure quality instruction in our schools?
- How do you feel about a Basic Skills Test requirement for graduation?
- What are the advantages and disadvantages of cooperative programs among districts?
- How do you plan to ensure that the school board (or supervisor) is informed of the issues and problems relating to your work?
- How do you plan to work with board members to reach goals?
- What are some advantages and disadvantages of having citizens' advisory councils?
- What is your role in the community? How would you develop community support for education? How would you keep the community informed?
- Describe the qualities you would seek in people whom you would hire to work in your district? In your school?
- How would you handle an administrator who was not effective?

MOVING ON AND MAINTAINING PROFESSIONALISM

A word of warning: Do not sign a contract until you have permission to be released from your present contract. Similarly, do not submit a letter of resignation from your current position until you have officially agreed to a new contract.

When leaving a position, professionals always submit a letter of resignation. For whatever reason and circumstances you are leaving, it is wise to mention positive experiences and professional growth acquired. One never knows what the future holds. It is smart to leave behind a positive message.

IF AT FIRST YOU DON'T SUCCEED....

Many applicants are not successful in obtaining administrative positions the first year of active application. If you are committed to attaining your goal and do not succeed, critically review your qualifications. Encourage feedback from others and seek advice. Build on your strengths. Locate areas of professional, academic, or personal weakness and begin working towards mastery. Along with realistic goals, add hard work, increased professional development, practice, perseverance, networking, and patience.

Whatever position you now hold, benefit fully from the experience. Accomplish goals, gain competencies, master skills, make positive contacts, and continually progress. To prepare for tomorrow, be the best you can be today. And, at all times, remain a professional. Professionals:

- realistically evaluate their qualifications.
- prepare accurate and effective sales brochures.
- maintain an up-to-date placement/credentials file.
- follow up on all activities.
- do their homework.
- are involved in professional associations.
- are involved in professional growth activities.
- let contacts know their objective, and request permission to use them as references.
- keep others informed of their progress.
- make each application a learning experience.

> *"The great thing in this world is not so much where we stand, as in what direction we are moving."*
>
> —*Oliver Wendell Holmes*

CHAPTER 6

Positions in
Higher Education

T he private and public institutions of higher education consist of community and junior colleges, four-year colleges, and universities. The job market in higher education is highly competitive, with an abundance of qualified candidates in some disciplines. The attainment of your career goal may be difficult and time consuming. Success depends on your efforts in taking full responsibility for completing all the necessary tasks in the job search process. A Ph.D. does not guarantee the J-O-B of your choice.

To maximize your chances of success, it is important to gain knowledge of the steps involved in the job search process. Spend time and effort in developing high quality, convincing sales materials. Create and implement an organized plan of action and thoroughly practice and prepare for the important evaluation interview.

Begin with an understanding of chapters 1-4, which outline the basic steps, procedures, and knowledge all educators need before entering the job market. Then proceed with the following section which presents the specific information necessary for an effective, organized entry into the marketplace of higher education.

INFORMATION TO KNOW

Self-Assessment—The Basis of All Marketing

In chapter 1, among other things, we discussed the importance of having a thorough self-assessment. This needs to be done consciously throughout life, but especially when entering the job market.

A valuable self-assessment is one in which you have seriously thought of yourself as a professional and how and where you see yourself fitting into your professional field. It also involves a complete personal evaluation of your unique qualities. What are your strengths and talents? Of all the qualified candidates, how are you exceptional? What distinctive qualities and abilities do you bring to this position and to your profession? How do you make a difference?

After all, in entering the job market, we have only one product to sell—ourselves. You have to truly know and believe in your product in order to market it. Even bright, capable individuals with exceptional aptitudes and impressive academic backgrounds need to be able to convince the employer of their abilities or their value may never be recognized.

Remember, employers do not hire the most educated candidate or the most prestigious degree. They hire unique, special humans—people they like, people who they feel "fit" the position and the institution. A thorough self-assessment makes you a more marketable salesperson and has the added benefit of guiding your search towards your right career fit.

Start by adapting the self-assessment questionnaire in chapter 1 to fit your situation. Then continue with the following list of considerations specifically designed for applicants of positions in higher education:

- Know the positions for which you qualify—based on your educational preparation and professional background.
- What kind of work do you want to do? (The employer will want to know.)
    Are you interested in working with graduate or undergraduate students, or both?
    Are you willing to be an advisor, or are you primarily interested in teaching?
    Where do you wish to focus your efforts—on teaching, administration, research, or public service?
    Are you searching for a full-time, tenure-track position? (There are many part-time employment opportunities available in higher education.)
- What are your academic, professional, and personal goals?
    Do you want to create a local reputation, a national reputation, or an international reputation?
    Where are you going with your career? Where do you see yourself five years from now? ten years?
- What type of institution will provide the opportunities to achieve your goals?

- Where, in what part of the country, do you want to work and live?
    What are your total lifestyle considerations, family and socialization needs, economic and political interests?
- What do you have to offer your profession?
    What are your strengths?
    What makes you special and unique?
    How will you contribute and make a difference in your area of expertise?

Know Your Job Market

Along with a continuous process of self-assessment, know the employment trends in your field of study. Professional associations publish this information in newsletters, journal reports, and surveys. College placement centers and faculty and administration in your department can also provide information.

In general, the higher education job market is crowded, depending on the field. The United States Bureau of Labor Statistics reports department shortages only in engineering, computer science, physical sciences, and mathematics.

The current baby boom is resulting in increasing numbers of elementary students, with secondary enrollments expected to escalate similarly after 1990. Nationwide, an expanded need for higher education programs and institutions is expected over the next twenty years. However, areas of rapid population growth are already experiencing increasing enrollments and anticipating the need for future growth and development. Throughout these areas there are plans for building new campuses, enlarging existing facilities, and developing additional programs and services.

Right now, a positive element in the college employment outlook is replacement needs. Replacement openings occur as people leave positions, either through transfer, career change, or retirements. Throughout the nation, large numbers of replacement needs are anticipated at the higher education level. Predictions say as high as 45 percent of the total college faculty will reach retirement age between now and 1994 in some areas.

In summary, the marketplace for candidates seeking positions in higher education is crowded, but there are opportunities. Those who succeed have thoroughly assessed what they have to offer, know what they want to do with their career, have completed all the necessary tasks, and have diligently applied themselves to the career search process. Others can assist you, but only you can make it happen.

Remember, 70 percent of your success in obtaining your desired position depends on your marketing abilities. (This includes accurately executing all the right steps at the right time in the job search process.) Only 30 percent of your success depends on your competency in your area of expertise. Those who are smart in their field are not necessarily smart in the marketplace. The formula for all serious applicants is hard work, planning, and preparation.

PREPARING THE PAPERWORK

Your Sales Brochures

Chapter 2 discusses the importance of developing and presenting effective, convincing paperwork—your sales brochures in the marketplace. The resume, business letter, placement/credentials file, and application form were fully explained and illustrated. Although the philosophy is fundamentally the same for candidates of positions in higher education, there are important differences in the required documents for this level.

The Placement/Credentials File

It is important for candidates of positions in higher education to maintain an accurate, current, and complete placement file (also called one's Dossier, References, Credentials or Credentials File). Most colleges and universities provide special materials and forms to best market your graduate courses, degrees, and professional experience.

Keep your file up dated with current letters of recommendation. Effective references for educators are professors, professional employment administrators, internship or field work supervisors, thesis or dissertation leaders, research directors, and leaders in your field. Refamiliarize references with your abilities and accomplishments, and inform them of your professional objective. Identify what kind of a letter is needed—an all-purpose one applied to several positions, or a letter tailored to match your qualifications for a specific position.

A Resume Or *Vita*?

Candidates seeking positions in higher education need a resume and a *vita*. Unfortunately, employers have no standard definition concerning these terms.

Consequently, confusion results when applicants find job listings with such statements as:

"Send Complete Resume" ("Do they really want a *vita*?")
"Send Brief *Curriculum Vitae*" ("Does this mean a resume... or maybe they want a summary or outline of my *vita*?")
"Send Full Credentials" ("Does this mean a resume or a *vita*?") (Usually this indicates the employer also wants a copy of your placement/credentials file.)
"Send Complete Papers" (Maybe a pedigree???)

Applicants often question if the hiring officials really know what they want. It hurts your chances of employment by sending the wrong paperwork. Therefore, unless a *vita* is specifically stated, it is advised to send a resume for the initial contact. Include a statement saying a *curriculum vitae* will follow if requested. This informs the employer you know the difference between the two, and are willing to send the additional information. When possible, call the official contact person to inquire which materials are desired.

The commonly accepted distinction between a resume and a *vita* is the following:

A resume is a one- or two-page document, commonly used by educators desiring teaching or administrative positions at the elementary or secondary levels. It is also often requested in higher education.

A *vita* is an extended and detailed comprehensive statement, providing a more in-depth, total picture of the applicant. It is appropriate when applying for positions in academia, research, or high-level government positions.

Step-by-step information for developing a convincing, effective resume is thoroughly covered in chapter 2. This chapter focuses on the *vita*—what it is, what it does for you, how it differs from the resume, and guidelines and suggestions for preparation.

The *Vita*

Although a *vita* is more detailed and comprehensive than a resume, its purpose is the same—to capture the employer's attention, creating a desire to invite you for an interview. A *vita* is also called a *curriculum vitae*, or a *c.v.*. It is appropriate for those possessing (or candidates for) doctorate degrees, and some master's degree level graduates, depending on their professional objective.

The length of the document depends on the applicant's background. A general rule is a three- to four-page *vita* for persons holding a master's degree, and a longer one for persons with doctorates. It is possible to submit a very appealing, convincing, and effective ten-page (or longer) document. No one is restricted to a specific number of pages. Whatever the length, be certain each word is carefully chosen, every statement supports your professional objective, and it is an informative, interesting marketing tool.

A *vita* is often sent in response to an announced position, accompanied by a letter of application. It also can be included with a letter of inquiry (although the letter-of-inquiry approach is not very profitable at the higher education level).

Most often, in higher education, the *vita* and cover letter take the place of the application form (which is used for initial screening purposes at the elementary and secondary levels). During the final selection of candidates, however, applicants may be asked to complete an application form.

Never minimize the importance of any required paperwork. A final decision could be based on the manner in which you fulfill this last requirement. All submitted materials represent you, become your sales brochures, and add to or subtract from your professional image. (See "Application Forms," in chapter 2.)

In higher education, applicants are screened, interviewed, and selected by appointed search committees. Most often, the *vita* becomes the critical document forming the initial and only contact the applicant has with the search committee. As committee members skim your *vita*, documents not presenting desired qualifications are screened out of the application process. Therefore, in order to proceed to the interview stage, it is vital to present a current, dynamic, convincing, and professional-looking document that is tailored to meet the employer's needs and fits the position.

Although a *vita* is longer than a resume and provides a more detailed description of the applicant, the two documents have more similarities than differences. (All candidates should study the resume section in chapter 2).

A *vita*, like a resume, is professionally typed, letter perfect, and attractive. It is an organized outline of your qualifications. It is written in concise, short statements, with little punctuation. Defined categories provide the framework of the document. Short paragraphs summarize the applicant's background and highlight accomplishments and suitability to the position. Like a resume, a convincing *vita* is custom made, focusing on your most marketable qualifications that meet the employer's needs. Therefore, you will develop more than one *vita*. Though they all contain much of the same basic information, each is designed to match a particular position.

Vitas vary greatly in style and content. Of course, every *vita* contains basic information regarding the applicant's identification, professional objective, professional experience, and education. The following list contains those essential areas and also includes additional possibilities for consideration:

IDENTIFICATION: Name, addresses, phone numbers.

PROFESSIONAL OBJECTIVE: (Same guidelines as for resume.)

QUALIFICATIONS or SUMMARY OF QUALIFICATIONS

ACADEMIC BACKGROUND: Provides more detail than a resume. List education (degrees earned or in progress), beginning with the most recent academic achievement. Follow with major areas of study, institutions, and dates of graduation. The following are possible categories and/or areas to include:
  Academic Background
  Academic Preparation
  Academic Training
  Academic Accomplishments
  Professional Preparation
  Areas of Concentration
  Areas of Knowledge
  Areas of Expertise
  Educational Background
  Educational Highlights
  Proficiencies
  Competencies
  Major and Minor(s)
  Master's Thesis or Project
  Doctoral Dissertations
  Courses (related specifically to professional objective)
  Principal Instructors

Highlighting courses and names of well-known or prestigious professors can be an effective marketing feature in a *vita*, especially for new graduates. Transcripts are usually not requested until the final selection of candidates. Presenting a strong academic background at the beginning of the screening process is advantageous.

CERTIFICATION: (If applicable) Include professional certification, certificates, licensure, and special training (as with resume).

PROFESSIONAL EXPERIENCE: Like the resume, this includes all full-time, part-time, volunteer, and temporary experiences relating to your professional objective. Describe the positions and department; include addresses and telephone numbers of employers, dates of employment, and names of supervisors. Carefully choose marketable category titles and list those experiences first that best sell you for the position. Describe responsibilities by using action statements and present specific examples of accomplishment-oriented results. These are possible categories and/or areas to include:

    Professional Experience
    Professional Background
    Professional Summary
    Professional Highlights
    Professional Accomplishments
    Teaching Experience (may include courses taught)
    Research
    Consulting
    Administrative Experience
    Internships
    Teaching/Research Assistantships
    Graduate Fieldwork/Practica
    Professional Service
    Faculty Leadership
    Committee Leadership
    Department Leadership

PROFESSIONAL ACTIVITIES AND ACCOMPLISHMENTS: This category may include courses and programs developed, grants, conferences, presentations, and other professional activities. The following are possibilities for grouping activities under this category:

Courses/Programs Developed: Include the name(s) of courses or programs, institution, dates, results or accomplishments from efforts.

Grants: Name, date, relevant data, and accomplishments or results.

Publications (or other creative works): Present the title and date. These are possible categories and/or areas to include:

Scholarly Publications
Published Research Reports
Essays
Books
Chapters in Books
Professional Papers, Articles, Monographs, Reviews
Exhibits/Exhibitions
Compositions/Arrangements/Scores
Recitals/Performances

Presentations: State the title of the presentation, and name of the conference, seminar, association, or convention where presentation was given. Include dates, and location. Appropriate areas to include are scholarly, conference and workshop presentations, and also convention addresses.

Professional and Academic Service/Involvement: This area includes academic and professional service, and university involvement. Include leadership positions, committee leadership or participation, membership on boards, offices held.

PROFESSIONAL AFFILIATIONS, ASSOCIATIONS, ORGANIZATIONS, AND SCHOLARLY SOCIETIES: Present names of current memberships (in alphabetical order). List offices held and leadership or membership on major committees. List conferences, workshops, conventions, and seminars attended. Include presentations, participation, and leadership roles.

AWARDS AND HONORS: Include with the education area or create a special section. Include scholarships, internships, fellowships, honors, awards, and distinctions. Grants can be included here or with the Professional Activities and Accomplishments category.

RESEARCH: Describe research projects in progress or recently completed.

SPECIAL INTERESTS/EXTRACURRICULAR ACTIVITIES: Include special skills, interests, training, abilities, talents, hobbies, language competencies, travels and foreign study, and special activities as they are related to professional objective.

CIVIC/COMMUNITY INVOLVEMENT (Include activities as with Professional Affiliations category.)

ATHLETIC PARTICIPATION/ACTIVITIES

MILITARY TRAINING AND EXPERIENCE: (If applicable)

PLACEMENT/CREDENTIALS FILE: State location of up-to-date placement/credentials file. This category can be titled Placement File, Dossier, Credentials, or Credentials File.

REFERENCES: Unlike the resume, this additional area titled References can be added. This includes a list of names, titles, departments, addresses, and phone numbers of individuals who have written letters of recommendation on your behalf. (Although this material is located in your placement file, it is beneficial to show names of references at the screening stage, especially if some are prestigious authorities in your discipline.)

Like the resume, there are many ways to categorize and arrange material within a *vita*. Carefully consider the layout of information and emphasize those strengths that are most relevant to the position. Each area can be individually presented or information can be grouped together. (For example, presentations can be listed separately or grouped with Professional Association Memberships.) Use the best arrangement and organization to market your accomplishments for the particular position.

Academic and professional status changes as one completes research projects and degree requirements, and as one participates in professional activities. A useful and impressive *vita* effectively markets current activities and accomplishments related to your professional objective. Therefore, it is very important to continually update information on your *vita*.

Two examples on pages 182-187 illustrate a resume and a *vita* written by the same applicant for a position of Professor of Spanish. The position requires instructing undergraduates and graduates, with research as an important job element.

Because the applicant is completing doctorate requirements and has limited professional experience in higher education, academic background is presented first. (An experienced educator may wish to present Professional Experience before Education.)

If the same applicant applied for a position as Spanish Instructor at a community college level, strong interest in research would not be highlighted. For a teaching position, teaching experience would be featured and teaching accomplishments emphasized. Of course, the Professional Objective would also match the desired community college position and other areas would be included to fit the position, such as community college teaching certification. This illustrates how one tailors the document to fit the particular position.

Of course, a *vita* is always accompanied by a personalized cover letter. This provides further details expanding on specific accomplishments related to the position, communicates strong potential in meeting the needs of the employer, and proves knowledge of the position, the department, and the institution. The *vita* and cover letter create a sales package introducing you and presenting your professional image to the employer.

Notice the *vita* contains much of the same basic information as the resume, but is more thorough, detailed, and comprehensive.

LOCATING OPENINGS

When Are Positions Advertised?

Although more openings are announced in the spring and late summer, positions in higher education are generally advertised year round. Vacancies can be published one to two years before they are actually filled. All search committees operate differently. However, new graduates need to be aware of the fact that the particular opening of interest may be published far in advance. The important message is that you need to be watching the marketplace activity for at least a full year before you are ready to apply.

By watching the job market activity, you gain knowledge not only of the openings, but also of how the job market functions in your discipline. Following employment trends in your area of interest makes you a more aware and knowledgeable candidate and therefore more marketable. This is a time-consuming activity. However, along with finishing graduate work, it is an important task. Serious applicants invest time and effort in learning about upcoming openings and gathering employment information in their field of interest.

Where Are Positions Advertised?

Many universities and colleges are tax-supported institutions, governed by equal opportunity and affirmative action regulations. Openings are published and distributed throughout the country. On pages 188-189, the main sources of job information for positions in higher education are listed.

Sample Resume

Lee M. Hamilton

UNIVERSITY ADDRESS	PERMANENT ADDRESS
333 Dunlap Drive	5000 Lakeview Avenue
Somerfield, WA 43434	Northbay, WA 43333
(912) 677-7666	(766) 877-7788

PROFESSIONAL OBJECTIVE

Desire position as a tenure track Professor of Spanish, anxious to work closely with individuals and groups, both undergraduates and graduates, in teaching and research where there is a need for stimulating teaching methods, including history and cultural understanding, aimed at graduating competent and confident language students—with the opportunity to continue research of Spanish cultural and contemporary events.

SUMMARY OF QUALIFICATIONS

Strong academic background and specialized training.
Eight years of successful teaching experience.
Practiced and skilled in research and publishing.
Leadership—Organized and planned student programs and activities.
Cultural awareness through extended travel and study abroad.

PROFESSIONAL STUDIES

Ph.D.: West Bradford University, June 1990, Spanish—L.Hawthorn Scholarship Award.
　　Dissertation: *A Generative Phonology of Modern Literary Spanish*

Master of Arts Degree: Dalton University, 1986, Spanish.

Bachelor of Arts Degree: Magna Cum Laude, Dalton University, 1981, Spanish major, English minor. Studied ten months at University of Mexico, 1980. Extensive travel in Mexico, and Central and South America during summers.

PROFESSIONAL EXPERIENCE

TEACHING ASSISTANT: West Bradford University, 1988-1989. Presented a series of lecture-discussion classes. Directed freshman study groups, resulting in increasing vocabulary and fluency. Involvement in numerous student activities.

RESEARCH ASSISTANT: West Bradford University, 1988-1989. Played key role in researching Spanish literature, history, and cultural events for Dr. Lazeres Guadalupe and Dr. Wilhelma Guzman. Material for Dr. Guzman to be presented at American Association of Language Instructors National Convention, August 1990, and also to be published in upcoming book.

EDUCATOR: Spanish Instructor, Portland School District, Washington, 1981-87. Developed individualized language lab program, significantly increasing students' fluency, grammar, and pronunciation. Introduced Spanish cultural studies. Directed Spanish Club. Left position to pursue doctorate studies.

Sample Resume *(continued)*

LEE M. HAMILTON   PAGE 2

PUBLICATIONS

Essay: "Teaching Spanish—Our Second Language," *Language Research Series No. 57*, West Bradford University, 1989.

Master's Thesis: "Teaching Spanish Through Contemporary Events and Cultural Understanding," *Journal of Spanish Education*, Fall, 1987.

PRESENTATIONS

"Modern Spanish in Today's Schools," presented at the American Spanish Studies Conference, Sacramento, California, January, 1986.

"Language and Literature," presented at the Annual Conference for Language Educators, Bellmont, Washington, 1988.

Directed Workshop "A Cultural Approach to Vocabulary Building for Spanish Instructors," Conference for Language Education, Long Island, Washington, 1988.

PROFESSIONAL AND CIVIC ACTIVITIES

American Association of Language Instructors, 1981-Present.
American Association of Teachers of Spanish, 1983-Present, Secretary 1988.
Modern Language Association, 1985-Present.
Honor Society Memberships—Phi Delta Kappa and Phi Delta Gamma.
Foreign Exchange Student Placement, 1983-1986.
Community Support for Scholarships Project, 1987.
Taft United Way, Board Member, 1986-87.

CONFERENCES

National Council of Language Instructors, Seattle, Washington, 1988.
Western Regional Conference of Spanish Instructors, presented by the Modern Language Association, Los Angeles, California, 1987.
American Association of Language Instructors, Scottsdale, Arizona, 1988.

PLACEMENT FILE AVAILABLE

Placement Service, 767 Reeves Building, West Bradford University,
Somerfield, Washington, 43434, (912) 765-0988, File No. 3344.

ATTITUDES AND INTERESTS

Strong interest in research of Spanish language, heritage, and culture began in childhood travels as the daughter of an army officer. Fulfillment attained when immersed in creative teaching activities that result in students' success and achievement. Find competency, continual updating of knowledge, enthusiasm, creativity, and dedication are the keys to educating.

Sample *Vita*

LEE M. HAMILTON

UNIVERSITY ADDRESS
333 Dunlap Drive
Somerfield, WA 43434
(912) 677-7666

PERMANENT ADDRESS
5000 Lakeview Avenue
Northbay, WA 43333
(766) 877-7788

PROFESSIONAL OBJECTIVE

Desire position as a tenure track Professor of Spanish, anxious to work closely with individuals and groups, both undergraduates and graduates, in teaching and research where there is a need for incorporating stimulating teaching methods, including history and cultural understanding, aimed at graduating competent and confident language students and with the opportunity to continue research of Spanish cultural and contemporary events.

SUMMARY OF QUALIFICATIONS

Strong academic background and specialized training.
Eight years of successful teaching experience.
Practiced and skilled in research and publishing.
Leadership—Organized and planned student programs and activities.
Proven abilities in group dynamics.
Created enthusiastic learning environments conducive to building confidence and mastery of
    competencies.
Extensive public speaking experience.
Cultural awareness through extended travel and study abroad.
Determined and formulated educational goals.
Evaluated concepts, curriculum, and practices.

PROFESSIONAL STUDIES

Ph.D.: West Bradford University, June 1990, Spanish.
    L. Hawthorn Scholarship Award.
    Dissertation: *A Generative Phonology of Modern Literary Spanish*

Master of Arts Degree: Dalton University, 1986, Spanish.
    Master's Thesis:*Teaching Spanish Through Contemporary Events and Cultural Understanding*

Bachelor of Arts Degree: Awarded *magna cum laude*, Dalton University, 1981, Spanish major, English minor. Lived and studied ten months at University of Mexico, 1980. G.P.A. 3.8, Dean's Honor Roll three years. Traveled extensively throughout Mexico, and Central and South America during summers. Financed undergraduate studies by tutoring non-English speaking students.

Sample *Vita* *(continued)*

LEE M. HAMILTON   PAGE 2

GRADUATE COURSE CONCENTRATION

Spanish History and Culture—Dr. Lazeres Guadalupe
Spanish Literature—Dr. Jon Hernandez and Dr. Wilhelma Guzman
Latin American Literature—Dr. Taylor Fellman
Spanish Cultural Events—Dr. Vera Pellemo
Current Events and History of Mexico—Dr. Maria Hartman
Advanced Spanish—Dr. Delores Medoza

PROFESSIONAL EXPERIENCE

TEACHING ASSISTANT: West Bradford University, 100 Hadley Way, Somerfield, Washington, 77888—(800) 777-9999. Supervisor: Dr. Robert Galtima. 1988-1989. Presented a series of lecture-discussion classes. Excellent student evaluations. Directed freshman study groups, resulting in significantly increasing vocabulary and fluency. Organized group to write articles on Spanish culture for campus newspaper. Involved in numerous student activities. Organized Spanish Club's "Fiesta Days" with great success. Led to other campus Spanish cultural activities.

RESEARCH ASSISTANT: West Bradford University, 1988-1989.
Played key role in researching Spanish literature and cultural events for Dr. Guadalupe Lazeras, 1988. Materials to be presented at Regional Conference of the American Schools of Mexico, Paseos, Mexico, 1990. Dr. Lazeras highly praised my research techniques.

Graduate Research Assistant for Dr. Wilhelma Guzman, 1989. Key contributor of material for Dr. Guzman's textbook, *Spanish History and Cultural Events for College Students*, expected publication 1990, Coldwell College Publications. Experience gave me invaluable knowledge in textbook writing. Materials also to be presented at American Association of Language Instructors, National Convention, August, 1990.

EDUCATOR: Spanish Instructor, Portland School District, 400 Seaside Way, Bayshore, Washington, (877) 876-9088. 1981-1987. Fairmont High School, Department Head: Barbara Dallman. Developed individualized language lab program, significantly increasing students' fluency, pronunciation, and grammar. Introduced Spanish cultural studies, with emphasis on literature and current events. Results: Strong interest, enthusiasm, and improved test scores. Directed Spanish Club, five years, increased membership 25 percent each year. Left position upon receiving scholarship to pursue doctorate studies.

(continued)

Sample *Vita* (continued)

LEE M. HAMILTON   PAGE 3

PUBLICATIONS AND PRESENTATIONS

Publications:
> Essay: "Teaching Spanish—Our Second Language," *Language Research Series No. 57*, West Bradford University, Washington, 1989.
>
> Master's Thesis: "Teaching Spanish Through Contemporary Events and Cultural Understanding." Published, Fall, 1987, *Journal of Spanish Education.*

Presentations:
> "Modern Spanish in Today's Schools," address at the American Association for Spanish Studies Conference, Sacramento, California, January, 1986. Rave reviews from educators.
>
> "Language and Literature," presented at the Annual Conference for Language Educators, Bellmont, Washington, May, 1988.

Directed Workshop
> "A Cultural Approach to Vocabulary Building for Spanish Instructors," Conference for Language Education, Long Island, Washington, February, 1988.

PROFESSIONAL AFFILIATIONS

American Association of Language Instructors, 1981-present.
American Association of Teachers of Spanish, 1983-present, Secretary 1988.
Modern Language Association, 1985-present.
Honorary Memberships in Phi Delta Kappa and Phi Delta Gamma

PROFESSIONAL CONFERENCES ATTENDED

National Council of Language Instructors, Annual Conference, Seattle, Washington, July, 1988.

Western Regional Conference of Spanish Instructors, presented by the Modern Language Association, Los Angeles, California, April, 1987.

American Association of Language Instructors, National Conference, Scottsdale, Arizona, March, 1988.

Sample *Vita* *(continued)*

LEE M. HAMILTON   PAGE 4

PROFESSIONAL SERVICE

Foreign Exchange Student Placement, 1983-1986.

"Community Support for Scholarships Project," fund raising, 1987.

Taft United Way, Board Member, 1986-87.

LANGUAGES AND TRAVEL

Excellent knowledge of Spanish.

Extensive travel in Mexico, and Central and South America.

REFERENCES

Dr. Guadalupe Lazeres, Professor of Spanish, Spanish Department, West Bradford University, Somerfield, Washington, 43434, (912) 765-0999.

Dr. Wilhelma Guzman, Professor of Spanish, Spanish Department, West Bradford University, Somerfield, Washington, 43434, (912) 765-0996.

Dr. Dolorez Medoza, Professor of Spanish, Spanish Department, West Bradford University, Somerfield, Washington, 43434, (912) 765-0993.

Barbara Dallman, Head of Spanish Department, Fairmont High School, Portland School District, 400 Seaside Way, Bayshore, Washington, (877) 876-9088.

CREDENTIALS/PLACEMENT FILE AVAILABLE

Up-to-date Placement File available from Placement Service, 767 Reeves Building, West Bradford University, Somerfield, Washington, 43434, (912) 765-0988, File No. 3344.

SPANISH CULTURAL AWARENESS

Strong interest in research of Spanish language, heritage, and culture began with childhood travels as the daughter of an army officer. As undergraduate college student, studied ten months at University of Mexico in student exchange program. Interest in Spanish culture continued with additional summer foreign travels to Mexico, and Central and South America. With completion of dissertation, plan to continue research and writing on Spanish culture and history.

TEACHING INTERESTS AND ATTITUDES

Fulfillment attained when immersed in creative teaching activities resulting in students' success and achievement. Find competency, continual updating of knowledge, enthusiasm, creativity, and dedication are the keys to educating.

Publications

The Chronicle of Higher Education is the Bible of information for four-year colleges and universities. It is the best single source for locating openings at this level. It is a weekly newspaper, normally containing about 100 pages. More than half is devoted to national and international articles. A multitude of topics are covered from current happenings, events, activities, research, deaths, promotions, grants, to basically what's going on in higher education.

Approximately half of each issue is called the "Bulletin Board." This area lists the openings in higher education. Large announcements are alphabetically and geographically indexed, smaller ones are arranged alphabetically. Nearly all universities advertise at least part of the time, if not most of the time, in the *Chronicle*. It is the most complete sole source of information on university-level positions.

Other publications for higher education job announcements include the *Affirmative Action Register*, the *APGA Guidepost*, and the *APA Monitor*. The American Association of Community and Junior Colleges publishes a vacancy list for those who are members.

Newspapers

For the most part, the community colleges and junior colleges do not use the *Chronicle* and seldom advertise nationally. They rely on community sources and college placement/career centers. Many times announced openings can also be found in Sunday editions of newspapers. Subscribe to the local paper in your geographical areas of interest for community college news and information.

Most universities seldom, if ever, advertise in a local newspaper. *The Wall Street Journal* and *The New York Times* are sometimes used on a nationwide basis for announcements.

College Placement Centers

Notices of openings for all levels of higher education are frequently sent to college placement centers. These are announced in vacancy notebooks, on flyers, and posted on bulletin boards. Sometimes announcements are sent to interested applicants through mailing lists. Vacancy notices in placement offices tend to be centered geographically, that is, university and college centers receive more announcements regarding openings from their home state.

The "National Association of People-Like-You"

Within your professional association there is a built-in paper network and a people network. Through newsletters, journals, and publications, you learn about vacancies, conventions, retirements, research grants, promotions, special events, and leaders in the field. Many associations provide job placement services. Often vacancies are posted at meeting places and conventions.

Becoming actively involved in professional activities provides an excellent source of information gathering and networking. More and more, employers are seeking people who show evidence of staying current in their discipline, and ones who actively take part in enhancing and strengthening their profession. It is to your advantage to attend, participate, and become known and active in association activities in your area of interest.

University and College Departments

Vacancy notices are often sent to deans, department chairpersons, and faculty in universities and colleges. These are often posted on department bulletin boards and outside individual offices. Stay in contact with your professors, and keep them informed of your progress and career objective.

For best results, use any and all sources of information for locating openings.

KNOWLEDGE ABOUT INSTITUTIONS AND POSITIONS

Postsecondary institutions have vast differences in size, philosophies, funding sources, academic prestige, history, reputation, and accreditation status. Student populations differ widely depending on geographical areas, academic pursuits, and career goals.

One of the most important elements of your job search is gathering information on the position, department, and institution of interest. This requires investigating, researching, and evaluating. By the time educators enter or complete a doctorate program, they have acquired numerous research skills. Use this ability to find and analyze information on your career area of interest.

This process of inquiry and analysis is necessary for two reasons. First, the information gathered is correlated with your self-assessment. You need to discover if this position at this institution meets your professional and personal needs. Is this where you will be an enthusiastic, motivated, and contributing educator? Second, gathering information provides the material needed to tailor your *vita*, cover letter, and interview responses. By proving knowledge of the institution and position, and by demonstrating how your qualifications meet their needs, you become a more confident and marketable candidate.

Begin your investigation by obtaining and studying a complete description of the announced vacancy. This contains general information, such as dates for application, name of the contact person, instructions for submittal of materials, and a description of the position. Many times this description specifies the special qualities, experience, knowledge, and abilities required. Use this information to launch further research.

Start with the college catalog. Campus libraries and placement centers carry numerous catalogs. You can also request one be sent to you. Become familiar with the philosophy, the goals, and the history of the institution. Read course descriptions.

Talk to people who know the institution. Friends, colleagues, college and university faculty and staff members, and associates in professional affiliations, are all good sources. College catalogs usually list faculty members, degrees obtained, and the institution where degrees were awarded. Find instructors who attended or graduated from your college or university of interest.

Research professors who are listed in *Who's Who In Education*. This will inform you of their backgrounds, talents, and specializations, and will possibly give you clues to the needs of the institution.

Local newspapers are an excellent source of information. Subscribe to newspapers in your geographical areas of interest to keep abreast of current happenings in higher education.

Visit campuses and departments. Gather as much information as possible about the position and the institution. What are the biggest problems facing the department at this time? Use this information to uncover how you might fill a need. Talk to faculty in the department. What kind of position is open? Advising? Teaching? Research? Working with undergraduates? Graduates? Is this a new or a replacement position? Find as much information as possible on how the search committee operates. Recently hired people are an excellent source.

Also assess the lifestyle of the total community. Does this location and environment meet your social, family, economic, and educational needs?

Chapter 3 summarizes information to learn about institutions, faculties, students, and communities. Much of the same knowledge is needed for an effective job search in higher education.

Researching openings requires an investment of time and energy. The more you know, however, the better prepared you are. Prepared applicants exhibit more self-confidence and knowledge, thereby increasing their sales competency in the competitive job market of higher education.

CONTACTING SEARCH COMMITTEES

Once you have researched the position and prepared your supporting documents, contact the search committee by submitting a letter of application with your resume or *vita*. The knowledge you uncovered during your research guides the writing of these documents.

Remember, the central theme of the *vita* is information. It paints a picture of you in an outline form. The business letter, in contrast, provides the personal element. It is written with the purpose of introducing you and your *vita* to the contact person.

Always address your letter to the specific contact person. Never address a letter, "To whom it may concern" or "Dear Sir." (See the section in chapter 2 on business letters.)

There are various directories in libraries and career centers to find correct names, addresses, and telephone numbers. *Paterson's American Education Directory* lists all educational institutions in the country by discipline, by geographical area, and by title. *Paterson's Schools Classified* lists institutions by disciplines.

If you have applied for a position and later decide not to pursue it, inform the contact person and search committee of your decision.

Because the job search can be a confusing endeavor, chapter 3 stresses the importance of having an organized plan of action, maintaining accurate records, and following through on all activities. Do not overlook these important steps in the process.

THE INTERVIEW

A thorough discussion of the critical task of interviewing was covered in chapter 4. Success in this sales meeting depends on your efforts in being thoroughly prepared.

Before the interview, continue your research on the position. If the interview is out-of-town, arrive early to proceed with your investigation and familiarize yourself with the campus, department, and community. This also gives you time to rest, be alone, prepare clothes and materials, and handle travel problems or delays. Bring copies of all materials with you.

Be prepared to accomplish your tasks. Anticipate questions, practice responses, and organize questions you may have uncovered during your research concerning the position, the department, and the institution. Learn about their future goals, intents, present priorities, and future directions.

Following the interview(s), do not overlook the importance of an effective letter of appreciation.

PROFESSIONALISM

Because every institution is different, search committees seek candidates with particular qualities that meet their individual and unique needs. Each search committee has its own method and criteria for screening, interviewing, selecting, and hiring. In the final competition, however, regardless of the institution, area of the country, or the exceptional qualifications you possess, all employers seek professionalism. Search committees believe that the traits candidates present during the screening and interviewing process are those they will also display on the job.

Applicants selected for interviews provide current and complete documents, write effective business letters, have the insight and interest to do their homework, and follow through on all tasks.

Candidates who are hired have convinced the committee members that they are their "right fit." They are prepared and knowledgeable, display self-confidence, and are genuinely interested in the position and the institution. They know who they are and what they want, and they clearly and confidently communicate their strengths, both orally and in writing. They exhibit professionalism in attitude, demeanor, and attire. The ones who are hired are actively involved in their professional fields and present a message of commitment, achievement, and dedication to whatever endeavor they undertake.

You always benefit by placing a high value on professionalism.

International Positions in Education

I t is easy to create a list of reasons why employment in a foreign country is an exciting and attractive idea. An overseas career adventure offers travel and exploration, the novelty of living and working in a new locale, the chance to meet and work with multinational educators and students, and the challenge of learning different customs and languages. Living and working in another country offers a unique opportunity to acquire firsthand, in-depth knowledge of the history and cultures of other peoples and nations, which is something a tourist cannot experience.

The majority of American educators who travel overseas to practice their profession also enjoy tremendous prestige and professional status in their foreign destinations. Although educators do not expect their profession to make them wealthy, the benefit package of an international career includes tremendous personal growth, expanded cultural awareness, and numerous professional enrichments and rewards. For many educators, employment abroad is truly a rewarding education carried with them throughout their lives.

There is another side to this seemingly perfect adventure, however. During their travels, most people experience some amount of frustration and unforeseen problems or surprises. Totally unprepared educators could find themselves stuck in a very unsatisfying, discouraging, and disappointing situation, or even arrive at the destination to find no job as promised. Their rewarding experience turns into a costly, exhausting, and frustrating lesson.

Therefore, along with the rewards, educators need to be aware of the risks involved and understand the special concerns and cautions connected with foreign employment. Living and working abroad is not for everyone, nor is it to be rushed into or taken lightly. Also, not everyone who wants foreign employment can obtain a position.

This chapter is not intended to encourage or discourage you from seeking an international career. Its purpose is to build awareness of the importance of thorough investigation, introduce you to resources and options, and provide knowledge for understanding the international career search process. This chapter is only the beginning of your research. References and resources are provided to point you in the direction of further investigation.

As with any successful endeavor, the attainment of your goal and the success of the venture itself depends on doing your homework. Start with the basic career search knowledge presented in chapters 1-4. Then proceed with the following information, which is directly related to those considering or seeking international careers.

INFORMATION TO KNOW

Qualifications

International schools seek highly qualified educators with excellent recommendations, with the personal characteristics and qualifications that fit the particular/specific needs of the employer and its supportive community. General standards for employment are similiar to those in the United States marketplace. (See "What the Employer Wants" in chapter 1.) Of particular concern for international employment is finding superior educators who possess the human skills, empathy, positive attitudes,and cultural tolerance to fit in and be accepted by both the school's faculty, its students, and the local community. International instructors and administrators have a two-fold responsibility. As well as being educators, they are also representatives of the United States and western culture.

Chapters 1 and 4 present the importance of self-assessment and understanding the employer, and they thoroughly discuss how to best present your marketable qualities in an interview. The following areas outline the specific qualifications and qualities employers seek in educators for international positions.

Academic and Professional Qualifications

Successful Experience. Because of the pressures involved in relocating to another country, generally, two years of classroom teaching experience is required. Administrators and other specialized instructors may need additional experience. Strong recommendations or references are a must.

Some international employers hire educators with less (or no) experience. These are usually in developing Third World countries, however, and can be a more risky adventure. In such situations, information on assignments and living/working conditions can be misleading or ambiguous, contracts may not always be honored, and positions may not be as secure. Before signing contracts for such positions, extra investigation is necessary.

With the possibility of limited health care facilities and the stress of relocation, retired educators are not usually as marketable. If you are an older applicant, understand your true motivations for seeking an international assignment. Then focus attention on convincing salesmanship of your professional accomplishments, suitable qualities and abilities, and unique talents and interests. Exhibit a healthy mind and body, a high energy level, flexible attitude, and enthusiastic interest in professional duties while gaining cultural knowledge. Submit excellent recommendations. These are not different from the qualities all applicants must present. Older educators, however, have an age factor working against them and must put forth extra effort in effective self-presentation.

Additionally, it is often difficult to gain employment if your area of expertise is in a discipline or subject not usually taught overseas. Many foreign schools do not offer extensive physical education programs, vocational or industrial arts instruction, or opportunities for special education. The needs of the employer depend on the purpose or philosophy of the school and its student body.

Advanced Degree. An advanced degree is almost always an asset, and may be required for positions such as administrators, librarians, and counselors.

Certification. A license to teach (or administration certification) in one of the fifty states is required.

Multifaceted Background. Academic preparation and experience in more than one subject or level is an asset to international schools. Marketable candidates are versatile. They can teach or manage in more than one area. Employers also favor those who participate in and show enthusiasm for extracurricular endeavors.

Bilingual. Speaking additional languages (other than English), or the willingness to learn, is always an asset but is frequently not required.

Personal Qualifications

When considering a foreign assignment, it is important to take extra time for an in-depth, objective, and critical look at yourself. Realistically assess your unique abilities and talents, professional accomplishments, and personal characteristics as related to an international career. Carefully assess your true motivations for seeking such a position. You need this information in order to make an intelligent career decision and also to effectively market yourself.

Review the self-assessment questionnaire in chapter 1, relating your answers to foreign employment. In addition, know your personal level of tolerance, ability to adapt, flexibility, physical and emotional health, independence and sense of adventure.

You need to know (and the employer wants to know) answers to these questions:

- What qualifications do you have which make you a good candidate for foreign employment?
- Why do you want to work abroad?
- Why do you feel you would be successful?
- When did you decide to seek an overseas position and what or who influenced your decision?
- What do you hope to gain from the experience?
- Where do you want to work? (Do you want one special location, or are you willing to work anywhere for your first assignment? The more flexible you are, the greater your chances of obtaining a position.)

Employers seek the following specific personal qualifications in educators for international positions:

Physical Health. A physical examination is usually required. Educators in foreign countries need to be physically healthy. Medical facilities may not be as accessible as in the United States. Climate, elevation differences, and living/working conditions may also need to be considered.

Independent. Singles and teaching couples without dependents are many times given preference. This is due to limited housing, availability of high quality medical services, child care facilities, transportation expenses, and moving of household goods.

Cultural and Political Tolerance. Employers want educators who are patient, open-minded, accepting, understanding, and respectful of the political and cultural views of others.

Emotional Stability. Relocating into unfamiliar surroundings can bring about a severe cultural shock. Emotional stability, an even disposition, a healthy sense of humor, and a positive attitude are a must.

Motivation and Enthusiasm. Employers seeking candidates for international positions look for highly motivated and enthusiastic professionals. This goes back to your true reasons and unique motivations for wanting to work overseas. (Obviously, it is not all travel and adventure.) Along with the challenge of experiencing new cultures, the desire for travel opportunities, and the chance to gain educational and personal growth, *motivation and enthusiasm for your professional duties is a crucial ingredient in selection.*

Flexibility, Independence, and Adaptability. Living and working in another country tests one's independence and level of self-confidence. For an extended period of time, you leave behind family and friends. You are now a foreigner. Flexible educators leave American customs at home, accept cultural differences, and willingly adapt to the routines and practices of their new environment.

Resourcefulness and Creativity. An international career tests one's level of creativity. Textbooks, school supplies, and video equipment may be limited in foreign institutions. You may have to make do, or better yet, have the initiative and ability to create enterprising, new ways of fulfilling educational objectives.

Spirit of Adventure. The motivation and enthusiasm for international employment comes from an inner quest to experience unique places and situations, and to meet people from all cultures. Those who desire an overseas assignment perceive living and working in a completely unfamiliar situation as a refreshing, exciting, challenging, and stimulating change.

Personal and Professional Concerns and Information Gathering

Because it is such an important decision, there are many concerns, special adjustments, and problems that need to be faced and solved when re- locating in a foreign country. You most likely will not have all the comforts and conveniences of home. Nor will you have all the luxuries we take for granted, such as television, communications, availability of grocery and clothing stores, banking and laundry facilities, transportation, fast-food restaurants, and medical care and supplies.

Success comes to those who plan and prepare. Before accepting or rejecting an offer, gather information on the country, the reputation of the school, the accommodations, and the living conditions. Your best defense against surprise is knowledge. Prepared professionals do their homework. They make intelligent decisions, based on self-understanding of their personal and professional needs combined with accumulated information.

When considering the areas outlined on the next few pages, create a list of priorities. Everyone is different, and each person has specific priorities and needs. Formulate questions and concerns to be answered and addressed. Your primary task is to be certain all your questions are satisfactorily answered before signing a contract. The more knowledgeable you are, the better you make an intelligent decision; the more favorable impression you make in an interview; and the better prepared you are for living and working in your chosen environment.

Chapter 3 covers "Information to Know" when investigating a position. The following areas also need to be considered before accepting a foreign assignment:

Contracts. Know the length of your contract commitment. Laws and customs are different throughout the world. Check to the best of your ability the validity of the contract and the ramifications that might occur should it be broken by the employer. Also take into account your current contract situation and what you are leaving behind. Are you guaranteed employment upon return? (Will this influence your decision?)

Country. Know the travel opportunities, climate, government, security, economy, language, religion, and the laws, customs, and traditions of the host country. What could happen should you deviate from them? Do you see conflict between your lifestyle and theirs? How does this country receive Americans?

Community and Living Conditions. Know the location and size of the community, type and availability of housing and costs, apartment leases, leisure/social/recreational activities, accessibility of transportation, standard of living, health care services, special health precautions, media and communications, and education for dependent children.

Position and Students. Know why the position is open. What is the philosophy/atmosphere of the school? Know the curriculum, number of class preparations, resources, supplies, facilities, and instructional materials (and how current they are). Know the type of students, ratio of American students to other nationalities, number of non-English speaking or limited English speaking students, and student/teacher ratio. Find out if there are extra duties involved and the availability of support personnel. What is the parent support and/or involvement in the school?

Transportation. Who pays for your transportation (and that of your dependents) and shipment of household goods for relocation? If it is the employer, then to what extent? Will it be paid in advance or upon arrival? If you return home for the summer, is it at your expense or theirs? Does the contract provide for other travels? What is the cost of owning/operating a car?

Salary. Once the hiring official has initiated the discussion of salary or a contract has been offered, make sure you understand the salary agreement. Is the salary and benefit package sufficient to maintain a suitable lifestyle? Have an understanding of the monetary system and what your salary buys in products and services. Is the salary paid in United States dollars, local currency, or a combination of both? Is the salary subject to taxes, by the host country or United States or both? How much United States currency, under the host country's laws, can you take out of the country when your contract ends?

Banking. Are suitable banking facilities available for both United States and local currency? Can you cash a check drawn on a United States bank? Can you easily send money to the United States? Are you able to use credit cards?

Visas and Passports. Do you have a valid passport and appropriate visa? Most countries insist a working visa must be obtained by anyone who wishes to be lawfully employed as an immigrant educator. Who is responsible for obtaining the work visa—you or the employer?

Information can be obtained through libraries, cultural centers and embassies, college placement centers, international education centers, and other educators.

Educators who are currently working in or recently returned from your area of interest are an extremely valuable resource. Career centers may be helpful in locating educators, or hiring officials may be able to give names and addresses. Talking and meeting with current or former international educators is a worthwhile investment (even calling someone overseas). You not only get first-hand, current information on working and living conditions and hiring practices, but you develop valuable contacts as well. As with stateside employment, personal contacts and networking play an important role in overseas employment opportunities.

Understanding the Marketplace

At one time, officials of international schools traveled throughout the United States visiting large numbers of college campuses to recruit educators. Many foreign countries wanted to prepare their students for schools in the United States or Great Britain. The American influence was at its peak and overseas opportunities for United States educators were excellent.

Today, the American influence overseas is reduced, and many foreign countries can now fill positions with their own instructors. Since international employment opportunities have decreased, the marketplace is not as active. Employers no longer need to actively recruit educators. Some international school representatives continue to visit a few favorite campuses and send out vacancy announcements to college placement offices. However, the majority of schools in foreign countries attempt to fill their needs through the following three sources:

Direct Contact. Applicants directly contact hiring officials by sending the required paperwork.

Private Placement Organizations. There are several private placement organizations specializing in the international market and sponsoring overseas recruiting fairs. These organizations do much of the initial screening of applicants and make recommendations to employers. They arrange recruiting fairs, located in a few central locations in the United States, so employers can more easily meet with applicants. These efficient, competent organizations have developed a solid reputation, and are strongly supported and used by overseas schools. They frequently provide other services to the employer as well.

University Placement Office Recruiting Fairs. A small number of university placement offices specialize in the overseas market and sponsor overseas and international recruiting fairs on their campuses. These are usually held in February or March, about the same time the private placement organizations hold their recruiting fairs.

STEPS TO FOLLOW

This section outlines the steps involved in the job search process and describes how applicants can best utilize the previously mentioned sources.

1. *Start early and gather information.* It is essential to understand the importance of planning ahead, starting early, and working diligently toward your goal. You need to begin your job search at least a year in advance. Applicants need to understand that competition is high for desired positions. As you steadily move toward your goal, be organized, patient, and consistent. (See the section in chapter 3, "Searching for the Right Position.")

   Identify geographic areas and type of schools of interest to you. Research the schools, the countries, and the culture. Match this information with your self-assessment and personal priorities as previously stated. This combined knowledge is important in making choices for application. Does this type of school, in this location, match your personal and professional needs, interests, and motivations? Can you adjust to living and working in this culture, in this situation, under these conditions? What further information do you need in order to make a decision?

   Apply for a passport and begin thinking about necessary arrangements for a one- to three-year commitment overseas.

2. *Direct contact.* Begin the application process by directly contacting headmasters and superintendents, or the organizations and agencies with whom you wish to work. Provide the following required information promptly in an organized, clear, and professional manner:

   A resume
   A letter of interest
   Three letters of reference or a copy of placement/credentials file
   A photo of the applicant (This is not done in United States applications. Passport photos are generally used.)
   Transcripts
   Verification of certification
   An application form (An application form may be sent to you upon receipt of above materials.)
   Some applicants send a video tape of themselves

   More information is included in an initial contact because of the postal delays in overseas mail and the long lead time in the international marketplace.

Along with the standard information addressed in chapter 2, your resume for international employment should highlight travel or study abroad, language competencies, extracurricular possibilities, and personal data. Voluntarily provide personal data regarding citizenship, marital status, number of children and ages, and spouse's occupation. This information is necessary because of the type of restrictions unique to international schools and communities. (You will also be required to provide personal data on an application form.)

Carefully tailor your resume and cover letter to fit the position. Begin with a custom designed professional objective matching the employer's needs and the unique community. Stress enthusiasm and motivation for overseas employment. Demonstrate abilities in resourcefulness and creativity, confirm a healthy mind and body, high energy level, independence, and interest in cultural awareness. Describe what you can do for the students, the school, and the community. (Never mention salary.) Meticulously follow the guidelines suggested in chapter 2 to create clear, organized, dynamic, convincing, tailored, professional sales brochures.

3. *Employment agency or international organization.* If you wish, enlist the aid of an employment agency or international organization specializing in the overseas marketplace. Contact them directly for specifics on registration. A placement fee (usually reasonable) is required for educators registering with these organizations. Get clarification of fees and arrangement of payment. See *International Employment Agencies* in the resource section at the end of this chapter for organizations and agencies offering varying types of services or information.

4. *Universities.* Consider registering for services and attending overseas recruiting fairs sponsored by universities specializing in the international marketplace. College placement offices allow graduates of any institution to attend these recruiting fairs. This is a perfect opportunity to meet the overseas school officials and gather information for application. Usually there is a small fee and a January 1st or early January deadline for registration.

Universities provide various other international career information and services—vacancy bulletins, referral services, international directories and data, and individual advisement. Contact each one directly for assistance and information. See *Universities* in the resource section at the end of this chapter for a list of institutions providing specific information on international careers for educators.

Other college campuses may also hold recruiting fairs, and can provide information about locations and dates.

5. *Your investment—time, money, and effort.* If you are a serious candidate for an international position in education, be prepared to spend time, money, and effort toward achieving your goal.

Be ready to travel, at your own expense, to overseas recruiting fairs held at several locations throughout the United States. It is possible you may even travel abroad during your job search, depending on your resources and motivation. Overseas telephone calls and postage costs need to be considered.

A successful international job search can take a year or more. In summary, the process involves making direct contact with employers, registering with a private organization, and/or registering to attend one of the university-sponsored recruiting fairs. The time frame for this process is September through December (usually a January deadline), for employment starting the following fall. Most frequently, in February and March, overseas and international employers visit the United States to interview educators and to attend recruiting fairs.

EMPLOYMENT OPTIONS

There are hundreds of foreign schools throughout the world seeking qualified American educators. The size and facilities of these institutions vary considerably from country to country. It is difficult, frustrating, and time-consuming for the inexperienced applicant to know where to begin, how to find information, and how to evaluate employment opportunities. In addition, there is no single office or one agency to assist all candidates.

The following are general descriptions of various employment opportunities for American educators seeking international positions. See the Resource section at the end of the chapter for lists of directories and contact information.

American-Sponsored Private Schools. These are schools that are or have been assisted by the United States Department of State. They are sometimes referred to as embassy schools. Educators in these schools are not employees of the United States government. Salaries depend on the location and size of the school and may be taxed by the host country.

The student body is made up of United States and Western European embassy dependents, children of employees of American and European companies operating in that country, and host national and international children. Although it is a multinational student body, the curriculum is typical to American schools and the ability to speak a foreign language is seldom required.

Many of these private institutions are college-preparatory schools with graduates usually qualifying for admission to United States or European colleges and universities. They are often established for the more prominent families, charge tuition, and educate the more academically able students. Therefore, embassy schools are not normally interested in special education instructors, speech pathologists, physical education, or agriculture educators. A listing of these schools can be found in the directory: *Overseas American Sponsored Elementary and Secondary Schools Assisted by the U.S. Department of State.* (See resource list for address.)

Department of Defense Dependents Schools. (D.O.D. Schools.) These are operated by the Department of Defense and were created for dependents of military and civilian personnel serving on overseas bases. The elementary and secondary institutions are located on or near United States military installations. Instructors and administrators are employees of the United States government. The staff, curriculum, and structure of D.O.D. schools are similiar to United States public schools. They hire all educators, including special education and vocational instructors. These institutions are located in twenty-seven countries and employ about 13,000 educators.

Generally speaking, employment by the D.O.D. schools offers many benefits over other overseas positions. Normally they offer salaries a little higher than stateside standards and in United States dollars (subject to United States income tax). They agree to ship more household goods, offer more frequent free travel to the United States, supply more United States products, and provide better health care. Educators are government employees and, therefore, can take advantage of military shopping and travel opportunities. Military housing or a living allowance is provided.

Most overseas employment contracts are for one or two years. At the end of the contract period, one returns home. With D.O.D. schools, however, it is possible (if one desires), to spend an entire career overseas. On a contract basis, one could live and work in many different countries. The military assists with housing, shipment of household goods, and possibly travel home once a year at its expense.

This is the safest and possibly the best choice of overseas employment, depending on your personal preference and motivations. Interested educators can request the booklet, *Overseas Employment for Educators* and obtain an application. (See resource list for address.)

Independent Private Schools. Many independent private schools for English-speaking students exist in foreign countries. Most are patterned after

American or European schools. Salaries vary with location and may be subject to host-country taxes.

Names, addresses, and descriptions of these schools may be obtained through various directories that are usually available in public libraries and university placement offices. (See resource list for four major publications.)

International Schools of United States-Based Companies. These schools are affiliated with large United States corporations operating in foreign countries and serve the dependent children of their employees. They are similar in organization to United States public schools, and all instruction is in English. Housing, furnishings, and transportation may be provided for educators. Salaries for educators are adequate to frequently very high (and some are tax free).

Numerous schools, however, are located in remote, isolated areas in developing or Third World countries. The probability of extra travel is slim and many times there are few social opportunities. Employers are usually oil, mining, and investment firms. Relocating into isolated areas can result in severe cultural shock for those not prepared. Do your homework. Before application and/or accepting a position, thoroughly investigate the locale, assignment, situation, and working/living conditions.

Interested educators should directly contact appropriate companies for information on opportunities, locations, and qualifications. Addresses are available in the *Directory of American Firms Operating in Foreign Countries*, by Juvenal Angel, New York Uniworld Business Publications, Inc. This directory can be found in public and university libraries.

Humanitarian or Charitable Organizations or Church-Affiliated Schools. Many of these operate in Third World developing countries. Assignments can be from a few months to several years. Some offer full salaries. Others, mainly service or religious organizations, provide only a small living allowance. The following international organizations offer employment opportunities for American educators.

Peace Corps. The Peace Corps offers career opportunities for educators in sixty-one countries in Africa, Asia, Latin America, and the newest location in China. Salaries are low, and in some situations teachers are volunteers, with living expenses and meals provided. Ability to speak a foreign language or willingness to learn is often required. Living and working conditions are usually low compared to American standards. The Peace Corps provides extensive orientation and training for their volunteers. It is a rewarding and challenging opportunity for those who fit the criteria.

Church-affiliated Schools. Like the Peace Corp opportunities, these are primarily located in developing Third World countries. Salaries are frequently low, and school and living facilities may be inadequate by United States standards. It is a rewarding experience for prepared and interested people. The ability to speak or willingness to learn a foreign language is often required.

United Nations. Applicants for the United Nations Educational, Scientific, and Cultural Organization (UNESCO), must have a doctoral degree and five years experience in higher education.

Other United Nations employment opportunities include the United Nations Children's Fund (UNICEF), World Health Organization (WHO), Food and Agriculture Organization (FAO), and the United Nations Development Program (UNDP).

YMCA. The YMCA Overseas Service Corps offers opportunities for educators in Japan and Taiwan.

Teacher Exchange. The United States Information Agency administers the Fullbright Teacher Exchange Program. This program generally involves a one-on-one exchange of American teachers at the elementary, secondary, and post-secondary levels with suitable teachers overseas. Needs and criteria change from time to time.

Higher Education Opportunities. There are numerous international career opportunities available for interested educators who are qualified to teach in colleges and universities. The Fullbright Teacher Exchange Program, previously discussed, usually offers professional or sabbatical exchange. Additionally, other opportunities exist for summer seminars, university lecturing, visiting professorships, and advanced research.

In summary, searching for and obtaining your "right fit" in the international job market is an extremely important assignment. A successful venture is not a matter of luck. It takes an investment of time, hard work, thorough self-assessment, in-depth investigation, and individual commitment and perseverance.

Successful educators reap the multiple rewards of their efforts and greatly enrich their personal and professional lives by using their profession to see the world.

RESOURCES

American-Sponsored Private Schools

Overseas American Sponsored Elementary and Secondary Schools Assisted by the U.S. Department of State. U.S. Department of State, Office of Overseas Schools (A/OS), Room 234, Washington, DC 20520. (703) 235-9600.

Department of Defense Dependents Schools

Overseas Employment for Educators. U.S. Department of Defense Dependents Schools, Teacher Recruitment Section, Room 152, Hoffman Building #1, 2461 Eisenhower Avenue, Alexandria, Virginia 22331. (202) 325-0885.

Higher Education Opportunities

Council for International Exchange of Scholars. 11 Dupont Circle, NW, Suite 300, Washington, DC 20036.

International Research and Exchanges Board. 655 Third Avenue, New York, New York 10017.

Register for International Service in Education (RISE). Institute of International Education, 809 United Nations Plaza, New York, New York 10017.

Humanitarian or Charitable Organizations

Peace Corps Recruitment Office. 806 Connecticut Ave., NW, Washington, DC 20526. (800) 424-8580, ext. 30.

UNESCO Recruitment. Division of International Education, U.S. Department of Education, Washington, DC 20202-6103.

United Church Board for World Ministries. 475 Riverside Dr., New York, New York 10115.

United Nations Recruitment Programmes Section. Division of Recruitment, Office of Personnel Services, New York, New York 10017.

YMCA of the U.S.A. Overseas Service Corps, International Division, 101 North Wacker Dr., Chicago, Illinois 60606.

Independent Private Schools

Directory of the European Council of International Schools. European Council of International Schools, Inc., 19 Claremont Road, Surbiton, Surrey KT6 4QR, England.

ISS Directory of Overseas Schools. International Schools Services, Inc., P.O. Box 5910, Princeton, New Jersey 08540. (Provides data on over 600 schools that employ American educators.)

Peterson's Annual Guide to Independent Secondary Schools. Peterson's Guides, Inc., P.O. Box 2123, Princeton, New Jersey 08540.

Schools Abroad of Interest to Americans. Porter Sargent Publications, Inc., 11 Beacon St., Boston, Massachusetts 02108.

International Employment Agencies

Association for the Advancement of International Education. Gordon Parsons, Executive Director, 200 Norman Hall, University of Florida, Gainesville, Florida 32611. (904) 392-1542.

European Council of International Schools (ECIS). Dept. PO. 21 Lavant St., Petersfield, Hampshire GU32 3EL, England. 44-730-68244.

Friends of World Teaching. P.O. Box 1049, San Diego, California 92112-1049. (Good for beginning teachers.)

The International Educator's Institute. P.O. Box 103, West Bridgewater, Massachusetts 02379. (617) 580-1880.

International School Services. Educational Staffing, P.O. Box 5910, Princeton, New Jersey 08540. (609) 452-0990.

Overseas Academic Opportunities. 949 East 29th St., Second Floor, Brooklyn, New York 11210.

Overseas School Services. Don Phillips, 446 Louise St., Farmville, Virginia 23901. (804) 392-6445.

Register for International Service in Education (RISE). Institute of International Education, 800 United Nations Plaza, New York, New York 10017. (212) 984-5412. (Computer-based referral system for college and university positions.)

Teachers Overseas Recruiting Conferences (TORC). Don Cermak, Director, National Teacher Placement, P.O. Box 09027, Cleveland, Ohio 44109. (216) 741-3771.

Teacher Exchange

Fullbright Teacher Exchange Program. E/ASX, United States Information Agency, 301 Fourth St., SW, Washington, DC 20547.

Universities

Ohio State University. B.J. Bryant, Director, Educational Career Services, 110 Arps Hall, 1945 N. High St., Columbus, Ohio 43210. (614) 292-2741.

Queen's University. Alan Travers, Placement Director, Faculty of Education, Kingston, Ontario, K7L 3N6 Canada.

Southern Illinois University. International Employment Service, Frank Klein, Coordinator, University Placement Center, Carbondale, Illinois 62901. (618) 453-2391.

University of Northern Iowa. Don Wood, Education Placement Director; Margy Washut, Program Coordinator. Overseas Placement Service for Educators, Room 152, Gilchrist Hall, Cedar Falls, Iowa 50614. (319) 273-2083.

Additional Resources

The following are excellent sources of additional information for educators seriously considering international and overseas careers.

Anthony, Rebecca, and Roe, Gerald. *Educators' Passport to International Jobs: How to Find and Enjoy Employment Abroad.* Peterson's Guides, Inc. Princeton, New Jersey.

Chesley, Richard. *Breaking In: Teaching in Private American and International Schools Overseas.* Addison, IL: Association for School, College, and University Staffing (ASCUS).

Connotillo, Barbara Cahn, editor, with Walter Jackson. *Teaching Abroad, the Learning Traveler*, vol. 3. New York: Institute of International Education.

Kohls, L. Robert. *Survival Kit for Overseas Living.* Chicago: Intercultural Press, Inc.

Webster, Steve. *Teach Overseas: The Educator's World-Wide Handbook and Directory to International Teaching in Overseas, Colleges, and Universities.* New York: Maple Tree Publishing Company.

Bibliography

Anthony, Rebecca, and Roe, Gerald. *Educators' Passport to International Jobs*. Princeton, NJ: Peterson's Guides, 1984.

Anthony, Rebecca, and Roe, Gerald. *From Contact to Contract: A Teacher's Employment Guide*. Cranston, RI: The Carroll Press Publishers, 1982.

Bolles, Richard Nelson. *What Color Is Your Parachute?* Berkeley, CA: Ten Speed Press, 1983.

Coxford, Lola M.. *Resume Writing Made Easy*. Scottsdale, AZ: Gorsuch Scarisbrick, Publishers, 1982.

Exchange: Targeting for Career Change. Fullerton, CA: California Career Guidance Association (CCGA), a division of the California Personnel and Guidance Association (CPGA).

Half, Robert. *The Robert Half Way to Get Hired in Today's Job Market*. New York: Bantam Books, 1981.

Jackson, Tom. *The Perfect Resume*. New York: Anchor Books, Anchor Press/Doubleday, 1980.

Lathrop, Richard. *Who's Hiring Who*. Berkeley, CA: Ten Speed Press, 1977.

Levin, Joel. *The Teacher's Employment Guide: How to Get a Job in Education*. Boston, MA: Bob Adams, Inc., 1987.

Michelozzi, Betty Neville. *Coming Alive from Nine to Five: The Career Search Handbook*. Mountain View, CA: Mayfield Publishing Company, 1980, 1984.

The 1989 ASCUS Annual: A Job Search Handbook for Educators. Addison, IL: Association for School, College and University Staffing, Inc., 1989.

Occupational Outlook Handbook. U.S. Department of Labor. Washington, DC: U.S. Government Printing Office, 1980.

Settles, Dr. Ivan L. *Marketing Yourself: A Handbook for Educational Administration Applicants*. Salem, OR: Confederation of Oregon School Administrators.

Sukiennik, Diane; Raufman, Lisa; and Bendat, William. *The Career Fitness Program: Exercising Your Options*. 2d ed. Scottsdale, AZ: Gorsuch Scarisbrick, Publishers, 1986.

Washington, Tom. *Resume Power: Selling Yourself on Paper*. Mount Vernon Press, 1985.

Additional Resources

California State University, Fullerton—Career Development Center. Langsdorf Hall 208, Fullerton, CA. (714) 773-3121.

University of Arizona—Career and Placement Services. College of Education, Box 307, Tucson, AZ. (602) 621-2546.

Index

Administration
    hiring process, 165–166
    information to know, 152–156
    interviewing/sample questions, 166–168
    locating openings, 164–165
    paperwork required, 159–164
        additional materials, 161
        placement/credentials file, 164
        references, 164
        resumes, 159–161
        sample resume, 162–163
    positions in, 151–152
    professionalism, 168–169
    professional preparation, 157–158
    self-assessment/knowledge of position,
        152–156
Application, letter of, *see* Business letters
Application form, 68–71
    definition of, 68–69
    guidelines, 69–70

Business cards, 76–77
Business letters, 57–60
    cover letters, 58–60
        letters of application, 59
        letters of inquiry, 59–60
    guidelines, 57–58
    information gathering, 91–92
    interview follow-up letter/sample, 145
    sample letters, 61–63

Certification, *see* State certification
Chronicle of Higher Education, 84, 89, 188
College career placement offices, 85
College positions, *see* Higher education
Contracts and professional ethics, 144–147
Cover letters, *see* Business letters
Credentials file, *see* Placement/credentials file
Curriculum vita, *see* Higher education

Directory of Public School Systems in the U.S.,
    86, 89

Employer, understanding of, 5–10
    what employers want, 7–9
    who employer is, 5–7
    who employers hire, 9–10

Higher education
    information to know, 172–174
        job market, 173–174
        self-assessment, 172–173
    institutions/positions, knowledge of,
        189–190
    interviewing, 191
    locating openings, 181, 188–189
    paperwork, 174–187
        placement/credentials file, 174
        resume/*vita*, 175
        sample resume, 182–183
        sample *vita*, 184–187
        vita, preparation of, 175–181
    professionalism, 192
    search committees, contacting, 191

Inquiry, letter of, *see* Business letters
International employment
    employment options, 203–206
    information to know, 194–200
        personal/professional concerns, 197–200
        qualifications, 194–197,
            academic/professional, 194–195,
            personal, 196–197
    marketplace, understanding of, 200
    resources, 207–209
    steps to follow, 201–203
Interviewing
    definition of, 105—106
    elements of, 110–112
    external and internal readiness, 122–125

follow-up, 143–144
follow-up letter/sample, 145
guidelines, 125–130
interviewer needs, 113–121
  on-campus, 86–87
  presentation needs, 113–114
  primary and secondary needs, 117–121
  professional needs, 114–117
  purpose of/tasks to be accomplished,
    106–108
  questions for applicant, 131–142
  questions for employer, 142–143
  sample follow-up letter, 145
  screening you out, 130–131
  self-confidence, 121–122
interview structures/formats and
  styles, 108–110

Job fairs, 86
Job market
  entering the marketplace, 10–13
    know your market, 12–13
    know your product, 11–12
    marketing tools, 12
    sales opportunity, 13
    steps for success, 10–11
  marketplace schedule, 3–4
  trends and projections, 2–3
Job search strategies
  locating sources, 84–89
    paper network, 84–87
    people network, 87–88
    resources, 88–89
  market research, 89–95
    information to know, 91–95
    letter of introduction, 91–92
  steps for success, 74–83
    budgeting, 82–83
    organization, 74–76
    plan of action/activity schedule, 77–80
    record keeping/activity accomplish-
      ments list, 80–82
Letters, *see* Business letters
Letters of reference, *see* Placement/
  credentials file

Marketplace, *see* Job market

Market research, *see* Job search strategies

On-campus interviewing, 86–87
Overseas employment, *see* International
  positions

Placement/credentials file, 64
  confidential *vs.* nonconfidential, 65
  contents of file, 65–67
  establishing/maintaining of, 64–65
  letters of reference, 67–68
Professional image, 147–148

Record keeping, 80–81
References, *see* Placement/credentials file
Resume, first sales brochure, 21–22
  accomplishment-oriented results, 30–32
  action words, 27–30
  definition of, 22–23
  guidelines, 24–27
  sample resumes, 54–56
  what resumes will/will not do for you,
    23–24
  writing resume, 32–53
    awards/honors/grants, 49
    category titles, 44
    certification, 37–38
    community/college involvement, 47–48
    education, 38–41
    ending, 51–53
    identification, 33–34
    military service, 51
    placement/credentials file, 45
    professional affiliations/activities, 45–47
    professional experience, 41–44
    professional objective, 34–37
    special skills, 49–51

Self-assessment
  understanding you, 13–15
  written exercises, 15–20
State certification information, 95–96
  state certification offices, 96–102
Substituting, 103

Vita, see Higher education